Army Life

Army Life

♦

The first four months in my first duty station.

Ramon Carrasco

iUniverse, Inc.
New York Lincoln Shanghai

Army Life
The first four months in my first duty station.

Copyright © 2005 by Ramon Carrasco

All rights reserved. No part of this book may be used or reproduced by any means, graphic, electronic, or mechanical, including photocopying, recording, taping or by any information storage retrieval system without the written permission of the publisher except in the case of brief quotations embodied in critical articles and reviews.

iUniverse books may be ordered through booksellers or by contacting:

iUniverse
2021 Pine Lake Road, Suite 100
Lincoln, NE 68512
www.iuniverse.com
1-800-Authors (1-800-288-4677)

ISBN-13: 978-0-595-37598-1 (pbk)
ISBN-13: 978-0-595-81993-5 (ebk)
ISBN-10: 0-595-37598-7 (pbk)
ISBN-10: 0-595-81993-1 (ebk)

Printed in the United States of America

Contents

Introduction ix
CHAPTER 1   June. 1
CHAPTER 2   July 27
CHAPTER 3   August. 49
CHAPTER 4   September 71
CHAPTER 5   October. 98

Acknowledgements

First of all I want to thank God for all the blessings he has bestowed upon me. Thank you for everything, especially my family. I know that I get out of line quite often, but I am working on that. You are my driving force, I have made it this far because of you. There is nothing I can do to repay you for what you have done. All I can do is believe, and I will strive to live my life according to your will. I love you God, and I give you all the glory.

I must say that I have the best parents in the world. I love you mom and dad, and want to thank you for your support. Both of you have a major influence in my life, and I am grateful for having you. I am sorry if I have not been exactly what you planned out. My goal is to always make you proud. I have tripped and stumbled along the way, but I will always get back up. I also know that both of you will be there if I ever need a helping hand. Thank you for always being there for me.

I want to thank my brothers Kevin and Victor, and my sister Christina. I love you guys. Thanks Christopher for making me an uncle.

If I named everyone in my family I would never finish. I want to thank every single one of you for your prayers and support. I have a great family, and I know that I can always count on you all. Thank you for always being there, I love you all.

Friends to me are very important. I have a few of them, but I have the best of them. Eric Garcia, Amber Zepeda, Vince Zepeda, Nichole Trevino, Jessica Perez, Justin Lozano, Cynthia Villarreal, Gabriel Galindo, Sheena Marie Dressel, Nathan Hopkins, and Jordan Parsons. Thank you for being there. You all played an important part in my life during different parts of my life. We have great memories, some of which we may not remember. Someone out there does. There a couple others who I would prefer not to mention their names. You know who you are, thanks.

Nikki Galarza, you always made me laugh, till this day you make me laugh. Thank you for always being there for me. I know that I have not always been there for you. That is not the one you want, do you. There were times when you could have used my help, and I was not around, I apologize. Thanks for everything.

Ali, I cannot apologize enough. I know that I messed up, and I will always carry that guilt with me. You were there for me when I first joined the Army. Your letters made basic training bearable. I am sorry that I messed up. Thank you for everything.

Rafa, stay out of trouble. I've learned not to take life so seriously from you.

Steven you are a brave person for joining at a time of war. Stay focused and do not let the negativity you may encounter discourage you.

Rebecca take care of your sister!

I want to thank Joan McCarson. You have been an incredible influence in my life. You are so talented, to say the least. I have learned so much from you. You challenged me as a writer, actor, public speaker, and artist. I am extremely fortunate to have had you as a teacher, as a mentor. My gratitude for what you have taught me is indefinite. I am a better person for knowing you, extremely lucky I would say.

Melissa Herring, I want to thank you as well for being a great teacher. I learned a great deal about writing from you. I was able to experience with different styles of writing. Writing for the newspaper and the UIL events have been very helpful. Thank you for everything that you did, and keep doing what you do.

Last of all, but certainly not least. I want to thank Victoria De La Cruz. Thank you for always being there, you are an incredible friend. We have been through some good and several bad times, but you have always been there. I am very lucky to have you as a friend. I thank God for placing you in my life. Thank you for sticking besides me and always knowing exactly what to say to cheer me up. I owe a lot of who I am to you. You will always have a special place in my heart.

Introduction

Army Life is a four month journal that details my experience in Korea. This autobiographical journal gives you my views on life in the Army. Life in the Army is different for everyone. *Army Life* only takes you into my personal experience and daily struggles. *Army Life* takes you into my everyday life, being off, my opinions on what I watched on television, training, being at work, to going out and partying.

1

June

Tuesday June 7, 2005

I have finally arrived in Korea! Looking back, leaving Big Lake was harder than I had expected. Coming to Korea had me a bit nervous since they day I found out that I would be coming here. I became aware that I would be stationed in Korea during AIT. AIT stands for Advance Individual Training. AIT is like going to high school all over again. It has the same high school drama, and the civilian instructors give it that high school feeling. AIT is were we learn how to perform the basic duties of our job, the remainder I will learn here in Korea.

Big Lake, Texas is where I grew up and graduated high school. There is nothing in Big Lake for someone with dreams and aspirations. We only have one grocery store, two gas stations, and one fast food restaurant. There is nothing to do there for fun. A Friday evening in Big Lake consists of looking for a buyer to buy you beer, if you are a minor. Everyone who is of age starts drinking early, and most likely will drink from sunset through sun rise.

Life in Big Lake is very predictable. You get married at a very young age, due to the expectancy of an unplanned child. You end up working in the oilfields. You live pay check to paycheck. You try to make a marriage work with someone who you are not in love with. The probability of cheating on your spouse is extremely high. You are more likely to win the lottery in Big Lake, than to have a marriage where both husband and wife are faithful. Being the talk of the town is unavoidable. There is nothing appealing about making a life in Big Lake, other than that the vast majority of my family lives there. Sometimes having all of my family there can also be a disadvantage.

I could never find fulfillment in Big Lake. My dreams and aspiration are to gargantuan to fit in the small town that is Big Lake. The predictability of living in Big Lake can be enticing for some individuals, not for me. I like spontaneity and taking risks. I have always told my parents that I do not want to live a normal life. I want to make things happen and experience everything that this world has to offer. Complacency can be a pitfall for success. Feeling complacent is a signal for change. There are those who listen to great stories, and those who make them. I want to be the character in the remarkable stories that are told, not the one listening to them.

While I was on leave in Big Lake, I avoided everyone as much as I could. I did not want to become attached and therefore making it harder to leave. My mom thinks that the reason I didn't spend much time with my family was because I didn't care to see them. That was not the case at all, I just did not want to explain that being there would have made it harder to say good bye. When my grandmother said good bye crying, it almost brought me to tears. I held my tears in, I did not what to seem unsure of what I was doing. Seeing me cry would have told them that I was insecure and unsure about leaving. They always thought I joined the Army for all the wrong reasons. I tried to seem as happy and excited as I could. I was happy about coming here, and to this point I am very excited about being here. I did feel scared and nervous. I won't be seeing my family for a whole year, I am not used to that. Me crying would have made leaving worse. I know my mom was trying to be strong, and me being weak would have made her weak. I kept myself together and held that knot in my throat. Men do not cry, I told myself. I love my family but being away is much better, at least for the time being. I'm away from the drama and chaos my family gets into. I personally do not want to be part of it or be involved in any shape or form.

Being here feels so surreal. I always imagined it, but once you're here it's a complete different feeling. It's never what you expect. It's so beautiful and green. There is so much vegetation and mountains, west Texas is complete opposite. It is more civilized than I expected it to be. I guess I was expecting to see what I've seen in the movies.

My mother was extremely happy to hear from me today. It took me twenty minutes to figure out how to use the damned phone. Even the pay phones are different here. It was the weirdest feeling to not know how to operate something I have always been familiar with. I had to ask the guy who was on the phone next to me to show me how to use the phone, using a calling card.

I hope my parents know I love them. I tell my parents I love them, but I also want to show them that I love them. To me actions speak louder than words, and here lately my actions have contradicted my words, questioning the credibility of my true feelings. There is an issue I am debating, whether to extend my tour here and extra year. This will generate more money for me, an extra three hundred dollars a month to be exact. This would be key to getting out of debt. I would have to sacrifice not seeing my family for a much longer time. My parents have asked me just to do one year here. I have thirty days to decide whether or not I will extend my tour or not. If I decide not to stay an extra year, it will be because of my parents. If I stay, it will be to satisfy my selfishness. Right know I'm really undecided.

I can't figure out how to turn on the damned lights. This hotel I am staying in is very elegant, I don't think I have ever stayed somewhere this nice. I even had to use my room key to use the elevator. Very technological. I will be staying in this hotel just until tomorrow, some one from the company I'm going to in Camp Red Cloud will be here to pick me up. I could not figure out how to turn on the lights or the air conditioner. I gave up and used the restroom with the lights out.

The other guy who is staying in this room just came in and turned on the lights and the air conditioner. It turns out that I had to use my room key in order for the lights and air conditioner to work. I guess that keeps people from leaving the lights on when they leave the room, therefore conserving electricity. The key has to be inserted into a small box that is mounted on the wall. The key has to remain there, and once it is removed the lights go out. Very cool.

Friday June 10, 2005

I was looking forward to running during physical training today, but since it was raining we didn't get to. So far being here has gone good, everyone seems to be very nice. That will probably change as time goes by. People always seem to hide their bad sides. Give them enough time, and they will begin to show their true colors. It never fails.

My roommate is really cool, he is from El Paso, Texas. So there is definitely some common ground, and the fact that he is Mexican just adds more to it. The day I got here he carried by bags up to the third floor. That was really polite of him. He seems to be too nice, people always take advantage of people like him. You have to know when to be nice and when to be aggressive. Some people mistake generosity for weakness.

I got to taste, well eat some Korean food. The food was delicious. I had some soup that looked like Ramen Noodle soup, except this soup had chicken and cheese.

I'm kind of bummed because Parsons has not arrived. It will be pleasant to see a familiar face. Jordan Parsons, is a friend of mine who I met during AIT. We are supposed to be in the same unit. I was really hoping to run into him during the trip over here.

Today all I did was in processing. It bothers me that I do not know what is going on. I had to wait about an hour and a half this morning before the sergeant came and told me what to do. I had to get someone to call him, otherwise the waiting would have probably been longer. The in processing consisted of going to the medical facility to turn in my medical file and fill out paper work. I also went to the dental clinic which is in the same building. They did not have my dental records, so I will have to wait until they mail the records to them to begin the in processing there. I also read every policy letter ever written. There was a total of three binders of policy letters. I had to read all of them. Some where repeated or just a different version, others were so old it was impossible to read them, and some where entirely to boring. Needless to say, I didn't read every policy letter in the binders. In processing can be extremely boring and tedious, but it has to be done at every different place of duty I am assigned to. I in processed in basic training, AIT, and know here. I will have to go through the same procedure when it comes time to out process. Out processing is still tedious. The fact that out processing is usually followed by going on leave makes it bearable.

I also was issued all of my NBC (Nuclear, Biological, and Chemical) gear. It was kind of frightening getting so much equipment. Hopefully I will never use it. The equipment I was issued is used during a chemical attack. I was issued a gas mask, which I didn't even try on, so hopefully it fits. There were gloves, pants, jacket, rubber boots, and packets of charcoal. Charcoal is what is used to decontaminate ourselves in case of exposure to any chemicals.

I was able to talk to my mother. It was comforting to hear her voice. I have yet to talk to my father, hopefully I will be able to call when he's back from New Mexico. I forgot his work phone number when I thought about calling him. Actually I couldn't think of it, cause I just now remember it, it's 650-2190. He wouldn't have answered, because it was one in the morning in the states. He would have been asleep by this time, unless he was at a bar flirting with the sluts that frequent such establishments. Since he's not home he could get away with being unfaithful. That would be extremely out of character for him though, he really loves my mom and I would doubt he would do something to hurt her. Maybe fifteen years ago he would have entertained the thought, but not know it seems like everyday that passes by the more they fall in love with each other. I am very thankful for my parents and the relationship they have. My father has never physically or verbally abused her. Plenty of children grow up watching their parents fight, I have never witnessed such behavior.

Before thinking to call my dad I called my grandma. I love my grandma to death, actually I love all my grandparents. I am closer to this one. Maria Luisa is her name, but everyone calls her Licha. She didn't answer, so I called Ali. Her sister picked up the phone. She told me Ali was asleep and I asked her what time it was and she said one. That's when I realized why my grandma didn't answer. It was kind of odd that she didn't offer to wake her up, she normally does that. Maybe because we broke up she feels it's no longer necessary for us to keep in touch with each other. She could have also been on the phone, because she didn't sound like I had just waken her up when she answered the phone. If she was on the phone she wouldn't of given it up to let me talk to Ali. That girl is always on the phone. It's as if she where born with a phone attached to her ear. She was probably talking to her boyfriend, and that's why she didn't wake up Ali, I think.

I completely forgot to mention that on my flight from Houston to Los Angeles, the infamous Ron Jeremy was on my flight. He also wasn't in the first class section, that was surprising. I always assumed that celebrities demand first class service every where they went. He could perhaps be a very frugal individual. Ron Jeremy is an incredibly famous porn star. He started out by posing for *Play Girl*, and later got into porn. I think I might of seen a porno with him in it once. He is known for having an extremely large penis. I didn't know him by name until he became part of the second season of the *Surreal Life*. The cast included Trishelle from the *Real World*, Tracy Bingham, Tammy Vaye, and Vanilla Ice, oh and Eric Estrada. I should have asked for an autograph, but when I first passed by him I wasn't sure if it was him or not. Now I regret not asking for it. How cool would it have been to have a famous porn star's autograph. He is actually fatter in person and really grunge looking. I should have talked to him, maybe he could have helped me get into the porn industry. Having sex for a living, what a living, granted I don't get any STDs or HIV for that matter. Other than that being a porn star would be awesome.

Saturday June 11, 2005

Jordan Parsons arrived last night. I was already asleep when he got here, but I woke up when he knocked on our door. I was really pumped to have seen him, I was starting to think that perhaps he would be going to a different unit. He also got married during leave, what a dumb ass, what the hell was he thinking. I guess marriage is all right if you have found the right one. The one you will spend the rest of your life with, but how is one supposed to know when you have found that person. For a while I thought Ali was the right one for me, and I was proved otherwise. I'm to selfish to get married, a lot has to be compromised, and honestly I'm not ready to compromise anything. There is still a quantity of things I want to do for my self. A very fundamental and enjoyable part of marriage is sex every day. That would be heaven; however that won't last forever. Being in the Army is extremely difficult for a marriage and especially here in Korea, because bringing the wife is not an option. What is the use. the only thing left do is masturbate. Fuck that shit, I'm not getting married. Unless I were to marry a local, but all they probably want is to make it to the United States and then leave my ass. Not to mention, as a soldier one will be away several times during our enlistment. That makes it easy to cheat on your wife.

My aunt's husband is in the Marines, and he cheated on her several times. Well once, no twice for sure. She really loved him, but he ruined what they had. Needless to say they are no longer together. In a relationship the couple has to constantly have to try and make it work, and that is not possible if the husband is always away. Eventually one of the two will fuck up, regardless of how much they are in love with each other. Shit happens, so until I can give my wife 100% of my time and attention, I will not get married.

Last night some lady got ran over by a military truck. She should have looked both ways before crossing the road. I don't know what kind of truck it actually was, but they say it's difficult to see what is directly in front of the vehicle. These trucks are apparently really big. Well anyway, we were informed by some sergeant that there will probably be a demonstration, which is a protest. If so there would be…I forgot the term they use. What they do is a loud alarm goes off, and everyone is supposed to get in their battle uniform. We also take all our NBC gear, and draw our weapons. We do everything that would be done if we were going to war. This was supposed to happen around two in the morning. This seems completely and utterly retarded to me, are we going to go kill off everyone who is protesting. I don't know much of how things work here, but people are allowed to protest. If they get out of hand there is the Korean Police Department, and the Military Police. Why would we have to prepare as if we were going to war? That is insane.

Thank God it did not happen, I was dreading it. I really did not feel like waking up at two in the morning on a weekend. Actually it wouldn't of been that bad, because I went to sleep early. I have a hard time sleeping after one in the morning. I tossed and turned the whole night. I guess I am not used to the time change. I always have a hard time sleeping when I go to a new place. I'll eventually get used to it.

I got to talk to Victoria today, that was great. She seemed to be very happy to hear from me. I also talked to Sheena and Gabriel. It was good to hear from them. Gabriel and Sheena are friends from AIT. Victoria, that girl is a whole different book on her own. Gabriel will be going to Japan on the 19th, lucky bastard.

Today I went off post to Uijongbu. It's so different. It kind of reminds me of Mexico. The streets are really narrow like they are in Mexico. Everything is really packed, the buildings are all right on each other. Cluttered and crowded is the perfect way to describe this place. I went along with Parsons and Diaz, my roommate. We went to an underground mall, it was enormous. There was a variety of clothing shops, more for woman than anything. It reminded me of a flea market, because a lot of the products they are selling are laid all over the floor. It wasn't like actual stores were you walk into the store. We also went out to eat to a small restaurant where they made pizzas. I had chicken and rice. It was layered with an egg omelet, it looked like a blanket covering the rice. It was really good, I added some Tabasco sauce to add some spice.

Sunday June 12, 2005

I am still having a troublesome time going to sleep at the normal time. A decent time to go to sleep would be around ten. Last night I think I passed out around seven-thirty and at four in the morning I was wide awake, but I didn't get out of bed until seven. I tossed and turned for about three hours. I finally got out of bed and took my laundry to get washed and talked on the phone while my clothes was getting washed. I talked to my mom, Victoria, and Nikki.

Nikki used to go to school with me in Texas, but she left our junior year to California. She was having problems with her step dad. She didn't know who I was when she answered the phone. It took her a while before she guessed. She said she was really soar. My mind went straight to the gutter and I assumed something else. It wasn't what I thought it was, she had liposuction done. She really didn't need it, she could have worked off the belly. She works with the doctor who performed the surgery, and he gave her a really good discount. He only charged her five hundred dollars, that's a bargain.

Tuesday June 14, 2005

I woke up very early this morning, because I had to go to Camp Yong Song, which is located in Seoul. I had more in processing to do. Turns out I woke up earlier than I had to. I was told we would be leaving at five-thirty in the morning, but last night around midnight a sergeant came and told my roommate to tell me that we wouldn't be leaving until seven. I remember my roommate telling me something, but I was in a state of unconsciousness that nothing was retained. I got ready entirely to early.

This morning while waiting to leave, I talked to my mom and my sister. My mother will be going to New Mexico this week to go see my dad. My sister says she's getting fatter because she's pregnant. Which is extremely logical. The way she talked to me was different, she is usually very cold and rude. Extremely apathetic usually, but today she seemed very interested in what I was saying. I guess motherhood is changing her. She even said take care and be careful, I don't think she has ever uttered those words to anyone before. It was a delightful feeling to hear her speak to me in that way. I know she cares, but this time she sounded like she cared.

I also talked to my grandpa and grandma. I didn't speak to my grandfather very long, because my grandmother didn't let him speak with me for to long. She was eager to talk to me. She was very excited to have heard from me. She said that she is always praying for me, which I really appreciate. I need all the prayer I can get. Once again she started crying, I don't like to hear he cry. She wanted to make sure I was fine and if I liked being here. I am fine and so far I enjoy being here. I always wanted to travel and see different countries and here I am. She said that as long as I was happy she was happy. That's funny because my father said the same thing. I think if I would have never left Big Lake I would have never appreciated my parents and my grandparents as much as I do know. I just pray that God keeps them safe.

People here drive exceedingly recklessly. Everyone here is a reckless driver. I do not think there is even a speed limit. They have no regards for traffic lights. They drive straight through red lights. One would think military personnel would be the ones to obey the traffic rules and what not. That is not the case, they are actually the worse ones. The sergeant who was driving ran almost every red light and drove very fast. I was somewhat nervous because I wasn't wearing my seatbelt. Just thinking that I'm going to have to get a Korean driver license and have to drive in the city makes me a bit nervous. The people on motor bikes are even worse, they weave in and out of traffic like nothing. They sneak behind the vehicles and pop out from no where. I am really surprised that there isn't more accidents.

The Korean police are just as bad, they are extremely reckless, and not because they are chasing someone. I have yet to see some get pulled over, which is extremely ridiculous. Almost everyone on the streets must have made several traffic violations. I really have not seen very many Korean police. The traffic lights here are weird because is not even a four way intersection where they are located. It is two way traffic and a random deserted street. I guess this justifies why everyone runs red lights, because it makes no sense to stop at a light when there is no traffic coming from the opposite direction. One of these days someone will come across and cause a major accident. The van we took to go to Yong Sang was extremely uncomfortable, luckily speeding here is almost a requirement.

Wednesday June 15, 2005

Today has been an effortless day. I'm just about done in processing, so I was released at lunch time. I've been watching television all day. Michael Jackson was found not guilty on all ten charges. I'm glad he was found innocent, whether or not he has homosexual tendencies and likes to molest little boys, I do not know and frankly do not care. Let that who is free of sin cast the first stone. I think the parents who willingly take their children to Michael, in hopes that some form of molestation will occur to gain monetary profit, should be the ones prosecuted. They obviously knew that he had been accused of molestation before, and to just leave their children with him is extremely evil on their part. I'm glad he is a free man, and may God bless him and renew his mind.

It still intrigues me that racism is such an issue. It seems like African Americans refuse to get over the fact that their ancestors experienced slavery and were prosecuted by white extremist groups. Today racism is not the case, but it seems like that is all they talk about. My God get over it, we can't always blame our misfortunes or mishaps on racism. that's such a wrong thing to use as a scapegoat. Quit feeling sorry for yourself, anything can be achieved if you set your heart to it. The color of someone's skin will not handicap the outcome. Maybe I just have never experience racism or known anyone who has been a victim of racism. It seems overrated to me. Yes, there maybe people who are racist against black people, but there are also black people who are racist against whites. Racist people exist, but no one race is the main race that is being subjected to racism. At least not know days. That's my personal view on the racism issue. I love diversity, it's a good thing.

I was watching a show were racism was being discussed. The discussion was between a famous novelist and a talk show host. Come on, what kind of racism have they encountered. They are obviously high class individuals, who are commenting and complaining about something the clearly have not encountered.

Thursday June 16, 2005

Today was a very interesting day. Yesterday we were told that we would be going on a ruck march, so for us to get all of our gear ready. The gear consisted of our kevlars, ruck sack, pistol belt, and LBV. Kevlar is another word for helmet, ruck sack is a bag pack, the pistol belt is what are canteens are attached to, and an LBV is a vest with ammunition and grenade pouches. Load Bearing Vest is the proper term. The LBV is also attached to the pistol belt, therefore; making it one piece of equipment. That same day Parson's and I went to the post exchange, there we ran into a sergeant. He stopped to greet us, and we made a comment about the march. He said to us that we would not be having the march, therefore; it wasn't necessary to go down to formation in all of our gear. Since we were told we would need the equipment we did not prepare any of it. In the morning on our way down to formation we ran into a specialist who told us that we did have to go to formation in our equipment. We ran back upstairs and made an attempt to assemble all that shit. By the time we got to formation we were late and forgot several items.

What infuriated me was that the sergeant who told us not to bring our gear was there with all his gear on. He should of said something to us that night after finding out that all of our gear was needed for training. I felt so stupid being late to formation, looking all retarded, because some of the equipment was not on right. It was horrible. I was trying to make a good impression, well so much for that.

Since it rained last night we didn't march to the training location. We rode in HMMWV. The High-Mobility Multipurpose Wheeled Vehicle was introduced to the Army in 1985. The HMMWV is four wheel drive with an automatic transmission. They can be configured to carry troops, shelters, and armament. The training location was on top of a mountain, that was the bumpiest ride ever. It was funny watching the facial expressions the other soldiers made as they were being tossed back and forth from there seats. I definitely had a good laugh. Everything was so green and verdant. There was lush vegetation everywhere I looked, some of which I had never seen before. Once we arrived at the top of the mountain the view was breath taking. The view was grand, like nothing I had ever seen before. I could see the whole city of Uijongbu. The clouds were resting on the mountain slopes, it was beautiful. Korea is a picturesque country. I just stood there taking it all in and remained silent. I did not know what to say, the view was absolutely incredible. It was not the same as viewing from the airplane. I guess because I could smell the air and feel the morning breeze caressing my face as I stood on the edge of a grand creation of God. Breath taking is the word, I was bummed that I didn't have a camera.

The training was about how to react to an ambush, and what to do when the key leadership is killed. I actually learned a great deal of valuable information. It was very interesting and educational. We did not have our weapons with us which limited our training. Our training would have definitely been more effective had we had our weapons.

Today is my grandfathers birthday on my dad's side of the family. I will have to call him and wish him a happy birthday. I feel bad, because I did not call my father for Father's Day. I had no idea when Father's Day was, I bought him something before I left. I knew I would be gone by this time so I gave him his present early. I would say that justifies not calling him on Father's Day.

Saturday June 18, 2005

Yesterday we participated in a company team development day. It started of by playing a game of softball and after that a barbeque. I am not a fan of softball, so I did not play. I just watched, which was actually kind of boring. The barbeque was fun, primarily because I was drinking. I had not drank in over two weeks. The dreadful entity about drinking is that it makes me want to be smoking. I really want to quit smoking, but when I drink I am fixated on smoking cigarettes. I let everyone have as many cigarettes as they wanted, that way I would not smoke them all.

At first I felt very uncomfortable, because I'm not the type of person that can strike a conversation with just anyone. I have always said that I will not talk to someone unless they talk to me first. I primarily talked to Parsons, and some dude whose name I forgot. He talked to me first. Parson's left right after the food was ready, but I stayed. I wanted to get acquainted with everyone, so staying would be the way to get to meet more people.

I have noticed that the KATUSA soldiers are very friendly and welcoming. KATUSA is an acronym for Korean Augmentation To The United States Army. They work with us separate from the ROK Army. ROK stands for Republic Of Korea. They say the ROK Army is really bad. They have to serve a mandatory two years in the Army. The ones who speak English take a test and if they score over seven hundred points they are eligible to come in to the Army as a KATUSA. Not everyone who scores a seven hundred points gets selected, they are randomly chosen according to how many soldiers are needed. They are extremely underpaid. When they come in as a private they only get twenty eight dollars a month. As they move up in rank they get more money, but I do not think it exceeds fifty dollars a month. This is a complete rip off. They do get free room and board, hair cuts, and they get one set of BDUs (Battle Dress Uniform) pressed a week. That still does not justify getting such a low income.

They do seem to be intimidated by Americans, they act very inferior around us. I think because they lack confidence when communicating. They say that they are better at writing and reading English. They struggle when it comes to listening and speaking English. Being a KATUSA also gives them the chance to practice their English. If someone does not practice a newly learned language, forgetting it is a possibility. I asked one of them what he thought about Americans, he said they were good friends. He also said a lot of them were bastards. This explains why they seem to be intimidated by certain people. It would not surprise me if they are treated different just because they are Koreans. To consider some one a bastard there has to be some sort of a negative experience involved. I have not seen them been treated unfairly, but then again I've only been here two weeks.

It's funny, because they all remembered my name and addressed me by it. I could not remember any of their names. Their names are so hard to pronounce, makes it easier to forget them. They tried to teach me some Korean, which I now forgot what I had learned yesterday. They said I have good pronunciation. It has been said that if English is a persons second language, it is easier for them to learn a third language. I would really like to speak Korean fluently, I will have to get the KATUSA soldiers to help me learn.

By the time the barbeque was over I really got to know more of the KATUSA soldiers. That is how everyone refers to them here. They are very genuine people, I can't say the same for everyone else here. It is going to be very interesting to see the rest of the characters here develop. I love to watch and analyze people. Very view times am I mistaken by the conclusion I make about people around me.

My cousin Steven left for basic training on the 16th. God be with him, because the first three weeks of basic training are the worse. I felt so alone and began to question whether or not I made the right choice by joining the Army. I questioned everything that first couple of weeks. It's a good experience, because like I said I learned to appreciate what I have even more. It might be harder for him, because he has never been away from home. I lived two years on my own before joining the Army, so I knew how to deal with being away once again. I have always been a loner, I enjoy being away and by myself. I am some what antisocial. I pray that God gives him the strength to make it through. My aunt could also use some help God, apparently she is having a difficult time dealing with the fact that Steven left to join the Army. I talked to my aunt yesterday and she said my uncle slept in Steven's bed. I guess that was a way for him to deal with Steven leaving.

It is extremely weird to see my uncle and dad show emotions, because when we were kids they really never showed any. For years my dad was a very cold person. Now he is incredibly different. When I went home we were all outside one day and my dad had me sit on his lap. It was so odd, I really do not know how to interpret that scenario. Sometimes I say, "why now." When my parents should have been there and showed love they did not. Know they suddenly become great parents. I've said "its to late." The past cannot be changed and expect for everything to work out just fine and be one happy family. I just does not work like that. For instance, I'm not home anymore, my sister is married and has her own life. They should have done all that when we were kids. My sister and I are no longer dependent on them. We have made our own lives and turned out just fine.

Even though sometimes I say, "why know when it does not matter". It does matter. It's the rebellious part of me that still exists, who says that. I love my parents, and I am extremely grateful for them. It is never to late to get things right. Our relationships with our parents are better than they have ever been. I think my sister would agree with that.

Back to Steven, he will have fun in basic training. Once he gets past those first couple of weeks he will be fine. I will have to write regularly, it made me feel better when I received letters. The times everyone got letters and I didn't, that really sucked ass. Everyday I looked forward to mail call. I think it was everyone's favorite part of the day.

Sunday June 19, 2005

Well it turns out that today is Fathers Day. I did not miss it after all. Right know it is still Saturday in the states, so I will call my father tomorrow.

Yesterday night was extremely attention grabbing. I was able to meet more people, one of which was in my same company in AIT. I don't ever remember seeing him. I also meat a female that lives down the hall. She was incredibly drunk last night. Generally when people get drunk they tend to say more than what they should. According to her there is quite an amount of homosexuality and sexual perversion with in the company. When I say homosexuality, I mean gays, lesbians, and bisexuals, all of the above. This kind of shocks me, because it is always the people we least expect. Well, other than a couple who are very obvious.

She also talked about this guy who apparently has any kind of porn out there. He provides everyone with porn. Turns out that while they were in his room a pop up came up on his computer. The pop up was of child pornography. The pop up video was of a child giving a man a hand job. That is revolting. Nothing out there bothers me when it comes to porn. All those weird people do that shit willingly and sickly enjoy it. When it comes to child pornography, the kids obviously are not enjoying it. That's sick, the kids are being subjected to something that is going to scar them for life. These kids life's are being ruined and sick people out there get off to that. His whole defense for having the child pornography was that one of the sergeants is into that. The sergeant keeps him out of trouble and he supplies him with child pornography. That is really low of that sergeant.

He is married, so I'm guessing he has kids. How would he like it if his kids were subjected to that. You have got to have a sick mind to find pleasure in child pornography.

It is going to be extremely interesting to see what other skeletons people are hiding. I have not been here two weeks and I know information I really did not care to know. I also know who to watch out for. My whole perception of that sergeant has changed drastically.

Monday June 20, 2005

Yesterday I went, with two female soldiers, to the "ville," as they call it. It is actually a strip of shops and bars. It is located right out side Camp Casey, which is in northern South Korea. The females I went with was the one who aired everyone's dirty laundry on Saturday, and her room mate. I figured I'd go with them sense I had nothing better to do.

Everything was considerably cheaper in the shops we went to. They primarily cater to women. They do have men clothing shops, but it is mainly hip-hop clothing. They sell brands like Sean John, Vocal, and Echo. Brands primarily targeted for the African American community, and anyone else who thinks they are black. Every other shop was a hat shop, they also had a large number of places to eat.

What caught my eye the most was the juicy bars. From what I've heard, these juicy girls who work at the juicy bars are primarily from the Philippines. They are contracted to work in these bars. What they do, is ask American soldiers to buy them a ten dollar drink. That is were the term "juicy" comes from, because the drink has some type of juice in it. In return they will sit and talk to them. Apparently these places are very frequented by lonely depressed soldiers, who are looking for a quick way to get laid. Turns out that a considerable amount of soldiers marry these girls, and buy out their contracts. The juicy girls are brought to Korea by means of human trafficking. Since the Philippines is such a poor country, they come here to work. They also come here in hopes of finding an American soldier who will marry them, and give them a better life.

As we were walking by these establishments, the girls stood outside the bars in very slutty attire. They left nothing to the imagination. So of course horny soldiers are going to flock to these bars. I was almost tempted to go there myself. Whether or not the juicy girls will have sex with the soldiers, I do not know. What I do know is that the soldiers spend a great deal of money for someone to simply converse with.

I've heard stories about the girls marrying soldiers, and once they get to the states they divorce the horny ass soldier. They start over on there own in the land of opportunity. To me it is very unintelligent to marry on if these girls and attempt to make her a house wife. It is completely ridiculous. She is obviously not a decent woman. We are talking about someone who is willing to exploit her self to get ahead. I'm sure there is a select view who do not fall in to the slut, whore category. Finding the select view who are truly there due to their circumstances, hoping to get out of the enviroment, to change their lives, and start over new, good luck finding one.

We also went to a bar, the entry to this bar was up a flight of stairs. It must have been really early when we went in, because the bar was empty. The owners were very welcoming. As I sat down on the stool by the bar, I was greated by an old lady. She placed her arms around my shoulders and asked me what I wanted to drink. I had a Corona which was five dollars a bottle. That is insane, I could have bought a whole six pack with five dollars.

This is were it gets ridiculous. The room mate of the other female asked me to buy her a drink, so I did. A ten dollar drink actually. Not only did she asked once, which to me was kind of forward to begin with, she asked three times. I bought her three drinks, actually I think a paid half for the third. That was about twentyfive dollars I spent on someone I was barely meeting.

Yes, the guy should pay for the girl's drink, but when I'm trying to get their attention. If I'm trying to hook up I will buy a girl as many drinks as it possibly takes, until the girl decides she does want to come home with me. Home, bathroom, car, anything will work for me, even an alley. I was not trying to do anything with her, she is not my type. As friends we take turns buying drinks. Me and the other female took turns buying, but with someone I do not know, fuck that shit. That girl had no shame. How can a female ask for someone to buy her drinks when they just met them? I was not going to say no, because I did not want them to think I was cheap. I had also paid for the cab that was twenty-two dollars. I figured that was enough. But wait, it gets worse.

When we got into the cab to go back to Camp Red Cloud, she asked to use my phone. I did not mind letting her use my phone. She did not talk on the phone for to long. Once we made it back on post, she asked for my phone again. Once again I let her use it. As we were coming into the barracks she stayed behind. About an hour later she comes into my room without my phone. I had to ask her to give it back. I had not used very many minutes on my phone. Here we pay for our minutes prior to using them, and it gets expensive. I did not want her using up all my minutes. That was very ghetto and disrespectful. Using someone's cell phone, that she recently met, to have a personal conversation with her booty call or whom it ever it was, is very ghetto. I do not think I will be hanging out with her again. Damned freeloader!

Today we were waken up at four-thirty in the morning, for a health and wellfare inspection. What they look for is illegal and prescription drugs. They also make sure we only have the permitted amount of alcohol. We are only allowed one six pack, one bottle of liquor, and one bottle of wine. They also look for cleanliness and neatness, but they are not to strick on that. The inspection was done by the sergeants. They did not search our room very well. If someone wanted to hide something they could.

I did not get to call my dad for Fathers Day. I could not find my calling card. I was also out of long distances minutes on my phone. I feel really bad. I should have bought a calling card. I was hesitant to do so, because I had that calling card. Pisses me off that I did not find it.

My friend Gabriel should be in a plane somewhere, in route to Japan. I talked to Sheena yesterday, and she said Gabriel was feeling scared. She told him to stop being a pussy, and get over it. She is very harsh with him. That guy is to sensitive. We get a kick out of being rude to him. He is a good person and has a good heart. I can understand him for being nervous. That's what is probably causing him to feel scared. He will be alright, I was nervous too.

I was told by a KATUSA soldier that I was cute. This completely threw me off guard. I really was not expecting that comment, especially from a man. I had no idea what to respond. I laughed and made an awkward face. He must have noticed that I was stunned by his comment, and said in his defense that he was not gay. I did not ask what he meant by that comment. I just left it at that. Koreans are different, because it is acceptable for two men to walk with their arms around each other. Perhaps it is also acceptable to tell a man he is cute.

Tuesday June 21, 2005

I woke up feeling like shit today! Not only did I get drunk las night, but got approximately three hours of sleep. I desperately did not want to go to PT this morning. When I found out we were running, I thought it was going to be painful. The run was at a moderate speed, and I felt really good during the run. I think my body needed that run, because I automatically felt better. I also thought that since I have been smoking I would have a difficult time running. That was not the case. I definitely need to quit smoking. The only way I can do it is if I quit drinking. The only time I cannot refuse a ciggarrette is when I am drinking. I want to improve my run time, not smoking will help I'm sure.

Today has been exactly two weeks since I arrived here, and two of the sergeants who I thought were very cool have begun to show their true colors. Parsons was put in the front leaning rest, (push up position) because he was persistant on knowing what the progress was on some financial issues he had. I felt sorry for Parsons, but it was truly comical. I had to try hard not to laugh. He was being some what adamant. Then he was asked to leave the sergeant's office. He was really annoyed by Jordan. I had begun to get up to leave as well, but the sergeant began talking to me about how money can be made by selling jerseys in the US. In the states they can cost over a hundred dollars, but here we can get them for ten dollars. I do not know if they are authentic or not, however; they look authentic to me. Ever so often he mails some home, so by the time he gets to the states he will have a nice stash of jerseys. What he will do is sell them for about eighty dollars. That's a lot of profit he will be making. I guess him starting that conversation with me was his way of telling me that I did not have to leave his office. I guess the sergeant has no problem with me, but apparently he does not like Parsons. I feel bad for him, because the sergeant was being rude to him. It was funny though.

There is one other sergeant who has given me the impression that he is a Christian, which was later confirmed. He has always been really nice and extremely helpful. He was a major part in helping me feel welcomed here. Today though, he was being rude. I had never seen that side of him before. Maybe he was having a bad day. I knew I would get to see people's bad side eventually. It was sooner than I anticipated. My first thought when he was being rude was, "and he claims to be a Christian." I take that back now. Just because someone is a Christian doesn't mean they can't have bad days. They have their moments when they are rude and my snap at people.

We all have our own battles and struggles. Everyone deals with their struggles in different ways, yet we are quck to judge and make preconceived assumptions. We don't stop and think that Christians are just like everyone else, we all struggle and deal with our own demons. The difference is that we turn to God and find our strength in him. We pray that he help us become better people and learn how to overcome what sometimes gets the best out of us. The worse, I should say. Christianity does not exempt someone from making mistakes. God can turn our messes into miracles. I should have not even had that thought, because I am no where close to being a good Christian. I have strayed from what I know will save me.

Thursday June 23, 2005

Yesterday we went to the range. I was extremely nervous, because I had not fired a weapon since basic training. That has been quite a long time ago, about seven months to be exact. I was expecting to shoot at pop up targets, but they were paper targets instead. To me this was easier because I was able to take my time without worrying about the target going down. I was able to concentrate and focus on the fundamentals of marksmanship. There are four fundamentals of marksmanship. They are steady position, aiming, breathing, and trigger control. The standard for qualification was to shoot twenty-six out of forty targets. I shot thirty-five out of forty. I was very thankful I did that well, because prior to qualifying I had only shot eighteen rounds.

I also went to a Chinese restaurant that was extremely good. The food was rather expensive, my ticket came out to about twenty dollars. It was well worth it. The food also gave me the runs this morning. My stomach does not handle spicy foods very well. I finally have gotten used to using chop sticks. Diarrhea is a small price to pay for a first class meal.

We went to some of the men's department stores, I was looking for shirts. The clothes was very expensive and not my taste. They say that the clothes here shrinks on the first wash. Like at the ville there was more of a selection for women, it is very limited for men. I guess men here do not shop. The fact that I have found nothing appealing, to me will keep me from spending my money impulsively on clothes.

Saturday June 25, 2005

Today I woke up at five o'clock in the morning. I was barely on my third dream when the alarm went off. I had previously volunteered to help Habitat for Humanity. a lot of us volunteered, but only three of us ended up going. We drove to Yong Song, which is in Seoul, and from there we took a bus. The drive to Seoul seemed shorter than it usually does. Normally I do not take my CD played but this time I did. Listening to George Strait made the time go by faster. The drive always varies due to traffic. Today the traffic wasn't that bad, that might also be one of the reasons the drive felt so short.

When we arrived we ate breakfast at Burger King. Eating there was much needed, the breakfast at the dining facility is not good at all. I find myself eating the same thing for breakfast day after day. Breakfast usually consists of a biscuit, sausage, and a bowl of grapes with walnuts and cottage cheese. Once we boarded the bus the drive was almost two hours. I dosed off, so it didn't seem that long. There were probably a total of thirty of us who went.

The place we went to was a rural area. The project was to help build homes. Once we got off the bus we walked to the location. It was about a five minute walk from where we parked. All of us had to use the restroom, that was the first place everyone looked for. We were told to take off our shoes to go into what seemed to be a recently completed home, that was not yet used. Let me take that back, it was used but not for living purposes. As I waited in line I noticed that whoever was walking in the restroom would slip on some sandals that were at the foot of the door. I thought this was weird and somewhat disgusting. To place my feet into sandals that everyone is slipping on, and God knows how many other people slipped them on, I was not going to have that. One could never know what people have. I would hate to end up with some sort of foot fungus. My mom always stressed never to wear other people's shoes. Once it was my turn to use the restroom, I noticed that the floor was abnormally wet. I had no choice but to put the sandals on. Actually I placed my feet on top of the sandals and dragged my feet, to make my way towards the toilet.

The reason the floor was wet was because the shower had no tub or walls. There was just a drain behind the sink that the water ran down into. The walls were all made of tile, so when someone showered there was no problem with getting everything wet. Why would anyone place a shower head with no walls around it? This is really messy because the sink and toilet get wet. Once someone is done showering I'm assuming they would have to dry off the sink and toilet. The water would also have to be pushed into the drain, because there was no downgrade to lead the water into the drain. That whole process seems like it would be a chore every time someone takes a shower. That would make me not want to shower, if I had to clean everything afterwards. I would probably leave it all wet and let it dry on its own.

After my complete amusement with the restroom we were separated into two groups, A and B. Each of them worked on a different apartment building. Each two story building consisted of four different apartment homes. All we had to do was cut the panels and hammer them from the outside, into the two by fours. This would make the external wall. There was not enough tools and equipment for the number of people who had volunteered. There were entirely to many people for the project, not to mention more than half of them had no clue what they were doing. There were two Koreans who were supervising our work. Everyone there however seemed to be an expert in carpentry. They all had a better way of accomplishing the task. They also criticized the construction workers, for their so called lousy work. These so called experts could not take the correct measurements. The vast majority of the panels that were cut, were either to short or to big. They should of just kept their mouth shut, because had it not been for the two Koreans we would have jacked everything up. Once the panels were cut an Army, literally hammered them in. There were about ten people per panel, all hammering away.

What really matters is the fact that we all got together for a good cause. Even if it was simply slamming nails into a wooden panel. It is definitely a good feeling helping build someone's home, someone who has probably never had a decent home. It's things like this that should get more media attention. The Army does a whole lot for the less fortunate. It seems like the only press the Army gets is negative. People are infatuated with hearing bad news or derogatory things about someone or something. It is a sick satisfaction they get.

The apartment homes were very simple. They were decent and definitely better than the rest of the houses around the area. The people there made us lunch, a very nice gesture. They had white rice of course, some cucumber stuff that I did not like, soup, and very spicy beef. The beef resembled fajitas, and the taste was very similar. I also noticed a big bowl heaping with Romaine lettuce. Everyone in front of me placed several leaves on their plate, therefore; I did the same. What they were doing with the lettuce was placing the rice and beef on the lettuce, and then rolled it up and eating it. Very similar to a tortilla, only it was a lettuce leaf. That is why Koreans are so thin, and the majority of Mexicans are overweight. Mexican food is very greasy and tortillas are very fattening. We should replace them with Romaine lettuce. The fact that Korean food is spicy really surprises me, I was not expecting that. I must say that the food is really good. To bad my stomach does not digest spicy food too well. Once we were done eating we continued working for another hour. After that we loaded the bus and headed back. It was a great experience, the people were very nice and hospitable. We could all learn a thing or two from them.

Today I received an email from my friend Gabriel, he is finally in Japan. He claims to be somewhat depressed, because he's away. Gabriel is having some girl trouble. He asked me for advice, I told him not to worry about it. If it is meant to happen it will all work out for him. He needs to enjoy his time in Japan and let God take care of everything else. If we would learn to place all of our anxieties on God, instead of trying to work them out our selves. We would save our selves a lot of trouble.

He will be fine, I think it's a normal feeling to feel depressed. Not only did we leave home, we also left our country. It can be very overwhelming. It is a whole different culture, language and environment. It can be very intimidating. We came to places where there are no familiar faces. At least Parsons is here, but Gabriel knows no one. I've lived on my own and experienced life. Believe me, live takes more than it gives. Gabriel is young. He has a lot of growing up to do. I'm not much older, but I've experienced more.

I also hope my cousin Steven is doing good. He has never been away from home either. Basic training can make a person want to drink bleach. God help him. Life in general can make a person want to drink bleach.

Sunday June 26, 2005

I woke up about ten-thirty this morning. I placed my sheets and comforter in the washer. Yesterday I washed my clothes, so today I folded everything and put it away. I was really bored, so I borrowed a movie from Parsons. The movie was *Collateral,* it was a very good movie, I had pizza during the movie. The pizza was extremely greasy, therefore; I only ate three slices. I was somewhat disappointed with the way the movie ended. I was hoping they would of wrapped everything up, instead the movie ended with no explanations on the future of the two surviving characters.

A guy from down the hall asked if I wanted to go see a movie. The movie was the *Amnityville Horror.* I had seen the movie while I was in AIT, but I thought it was worth watching it again. Parsons also went with us and some other guy from the company was there. Once the movie was over we exited the theater, and it was raining. It was quite a walk from the theater to the barracks. During our walk we argued whether or not the movie was a factual event. Yes, it's based on a true story, but that does not mean everything that happened in the movie happened in real life. Hollywood always stretches the truth and glorifies the facts to a great extent.

Then the conversation diverted to religion. One should never discuss religion or politics in a group because someone will always get offended. The only way no one will get butt hurt is if everyone involved in the conversaton is of the same faith and political background, which is never the case. Luckily the walk was not far enough for the conversation to escalate any further than what it needed to. Once we made it inside the barracks everyone went into their rooms, and the conversation was over.

I feel really bad, because I have not been going to church. We are very secluded here so going to church is not that easy. They do have church services here, but I am not sure what religion the services are. I will have to look more into that. I cannot aford missing church, I am a lost soul. I need guidance and spiritual nourishment, otherwise I will loose my sanity. There is very little of that left. I'm in the Army for God's sake. I always said that I would never join the Army. Joining the Army was definitely last resort for me. I tried going to school, which worked out fine the first semester. Once I singed my modeling contract with OTM, school was no longer important. Boy was I wrong, the only job I got from that contract was a two day job promoting Wriggles, longer lasting, Spearmint Gum. I also singed with Avant Models & Casting Inc., which did nothing for me either. I had a really good job in San Antonio, with Clarke American check printers. I got fired from there. I would call into work every time I had an audition, I exhausted the time allowed to be absent and they fired me. My car also broke down and I ended up back in Big Lake.

In Big Lake I got a job working as a jailor at the local county prison. That has definitely been my favorite job till this day. Victoria also worked there as a dispatcher. Going to work with her made it enjoyable. We had a plethora of good times working together. People there, however; talked to much shit. They loved to gossip, and the worse ones were the grown men. They were always out to get someone in trouble. Everyone seemed to always be interested in getting involved, commenting, and even making up shit about people's life. Ridiculous best describes the environment at work. They all talked behind each others back. When they were confronted they always denied everything. Damned cowards!

Victoria and I decided we had been there long enough. We did not want to end up like everyone else and stay in Big Lake forever. We headed back to San Antonio. She went to stay with her twin sister Rebecca, and I stayed with my aunt Karina. I could not find a decent job the three months I lived there, so I went back to Big Lake.

That spring I worked at Old Navy in Midland. My plan consisted of going back to school in the fall. Midland College accepted my enrollment application. I drove back and forth from Midland to Big Lake. I was going to continue doing so until the house I was going to move in was ready. On my way to work one morning I hit a deer and totaled my car. Once again I found myself without a vehicle. My only choice was to work in oilfield construction, there in Big Lake until the fall. I had planed, that once school started my car would be fixed and I would be ready to move to Midland.

The only way I could afford going to college was to get financial aid. My sister and I both applied for financial aid. We both were denied, apparently my father makes enough money to send the both of us to college. He sent me to college while I lived in San Antonio, but the two of us was not going to happen. I was forced to continue working in oilfield construction. I later began working as an assistant pumper, for someone who was physically injured. The money was good and the physical work very minimal. I stared dating Ali, and getting out of my credit card debt became more existent. I could have gotten a loan to go to school, but I did not want to owe more than I already did. Things were going good, I was living a normal and safe life. Living the role everyone in Big Lake lives. I was becoming what I had always dreded, to be content with my life and end up staying in Big Lake, like everyone else. I had ran out of options, so the Army was my last resort. I had always said that if they started the draft my ass was going to Mexico. "I'm never joining the Army, fuck no!" I found myself eating my words. Now I know why they say never say never. So here I am, and so far its been good. I'm in a different country. I always wanted to travel and I'm doing plenty of that. The pay is not bad, and I'm doing a lot of things I've never done before. The Army has been beneficial to me, so far.

I believe that everything happens for a reason. There has to be a reason why everything I tried out did not work. The Army seems to be working out so far. Perhaps I was destined to be an United States Army soldier. That sounds very weird. I never saw myself as a soldier. I always imagined myself doing many different things, but this one was not one of them. My senior year in high school I planned everything out. It was nothing like this. Life has a funny way of changing your plans. As long as I'm here I will make the best of it.

Tomorrow will be a slack day. We have a three day weekend, so I will be able to sleep in. I love to sleep.

Monday June 27, 2005

Today, definitely a slack day. Just like I had predicted it. Once I managed to get out of bed I watched the movie *Saw*. Extraordinary movie, with a genius plot. The ending, complete surprise. I give this movie two thumbs up. It is so crazy that people can watch movies before they are out on DVD. I would never buy a pirated copy. Pirated copies are definitely not the same as having the lagitamate DVD, I like all the extras that they come with. The same thing with CD's, I perfer buying the real deal. I also watched the movie *Mind Hunters,* an extremely perfect movie. The plot was incredible, and it also had a surprise ending. It kept me guessing untill the very end. Definitely a must see movie.

We did have to sweep, mop, and wax the hallway, but that wasn't a big deal. Right now I am watching cable, got it today. I am also enjoying a Bud Light. I do not plan to drink to much, because tomorrow I will have to go to PT. I will drink moderately.

Tuesday June 28, 2005

I am extremely glad that I did not get drunk last night. We were woken up at approximately four in the morning. We had an alert, which was the word I could not remember days ago. We had to get in all of our battle gear and draw our weapons. It's a simulation of war, in case North Korea attacks. We will be prepared. Yeah right. Once we got our weapons all we did was stand there until about eight thiry in the morning. This was completely ridiculous. What is the purpose of going through the whole simulation of getting prepared for a possible attack, just to stand there with no direction. Completely unorganized, had this been a real life situation I would have been dead as well as everyone else. This is kind of frightful. I can picture the whole situation being chaotic, in a real setting. If we are going to be waken up so freaking early, might as well do something productive. Something that will helps us in case of a real attack. I really hate standing there not knowing what the hell is goin on.

In the midst of the mass chaos, I called home. No one answered, so I called the cell phone. My parents and brothers were on their way to New Mexico, for vacation. We never went on a vacation when my sister and I were kids. The only remote thing to a vacation was when we went to my aunt and uncles ranch in Mexico. Yeah it was fun, but I would have liked to go other places. We went very often, usually during Christmas. I would always spend the summers there as well. My mom always hated going there, because it was never a vacation for her. All she did was cook. Her and my aunt would cook three meals a day. They were extremely delicious, but my mom hated leaving home only to cook else where. I am glad they are getting out more, my father usually never liked to go anywhere else other than Mexico. Any chance he gets he goes to Mexico.

Well it turns out that my cousin who recently turned seventeem, eloped with her boyfriend. Apparently she is pregnant. I thought Jocelyn would have learned from her sister's mistakes. My sister had plenty of examples by which to have made the decision of not getting married and pregnant so young. My aunts who did so all lived through very difficult situations. They were all abused and beat by their husbands. They are divorced now. You would think after witnessing such malignant marriages, she would have waited to get married. What is the big hurry, I do not understand. If love if meant to be forever, there is no sense in rushing it. Forever is a long time, long enough to take things calm and slow. Having a kid puts your life on pause. There is so many things to do and see in this world. Why cut yourself short. I have to many goals and aspirations to decide and start a family. I am not that young, so even if I decided to have a family it would be okay. I still don't feel like I am ready. I just hope this guy gives my cousin a good life and treats her good. I also hope she finshess school. I give my sister props for at least waiting until she graduated to get married, nineteen years is not as bad as seventeen.

My dad tells me that my uncle still cries, because Steven left to join the Army. This surprises me inmensly. I have never seen that man cry. My dad tends to exaggerate, I do not know how true that may be. My dad told me that my uncle said he did not know how much he actually loved his kids. That he did not know he loved them that much. You do not know what you have until its gone. Steven is not gone but he is away. My dad was even surprised to see my uncle so affected by the fact that Steven left to join the Army. I think that my dad is the more sensitive out of his two brothers. I guess because I lived with him, and I know him better. My dad did not cry when I left. Then again I had been gone before. My dad has always supported my decisions. I don't think my uncle supported Steven's decision to join the Army. Perhaps because of everything that is going on in the Middle East. It would be hard for any parent.

Wednesday June 29, 2005

Last night Gabriel called me, he is extremely disappointed with Sheena. He says that every time he calls her she is to busy or sleeping, so they do not talk for to long. The times they do talk all she talks about is her ex-boyfriend. She might be doing that to push Gabriel away and save him the heartache. Gabriel was really into her, and know is apathetic about having a future with her. I think it's better that way, he is to much of a nice guy for her. He felt he was having to change who he is to establish some common ground with her. Sheena is very unpredictable and Gabriel always plays it safe.

Today our new first sergeant took command. The fisrt sergeant we had was alright I guess. I did not know him long enough to make a judgement on whether or not he was a good NCO. He was only a first sergeant four months. The one prior to him was relieved from duty, due to some sexual harassment issues. I really do not know the details. The new first sergeant seems cool, I get a good vibe from him. We will see.

Thursday June 30, 2005

My sister woke me up extremely early today. Around four-twenty this morning my phone started ringing. I told her I would call her back once I got up. I was really surprised she called, I liked that though. I'm usually the one always calling, a good change for her to call. Once again it shows that she cares, my sister hardly ever shows she cares. She seems to be doing good. I am very excited about being an uncle. I am going to spoil the hell out of that baby.

Every Thursday morning it's sergeant time. From seven-thirty to eleven-thirty it is mandatory sergeant time training. What is odd, is that a specialist not a sergeant has done the training twice since I've been here. One week it is MOS training and the other will be tactical training, rotating every other week. This week the training was on reacting to an ambush, we had our weapons this time so it was more effective. I must say it was quite interesting and fun. Normally any type of training is boring. I had to leave early, because I had to go to Yong Song for an EO class. It was primarily about sexual assault, harassment, and rape. Apparently the Army has a rising number of these cases. We just can't learn to keep our dicks in our pants. If anyone is that horny that they feel they have to rape someone to get satisfied, there is something mentally wrong there. It is not worth loosing a carrer over minutes of pleasure. Dude, just masturbate, much saver. This class is given every month, and every month the statistics increase. Soldiers love sex, and look for it in the wrong places. What is this world coming to?

Today I also forgot my identification card. When I got to the gate at Yong Song I noticed I did not have my identification card. Everyone else handed their identification cards to the security guard, he scanned them, and handed them right back. He never asked for mine. I entered and exited the gates a total of four times, and not once did they ask for mine. That is kind of scary, anyone could get on base without and identification card. Security is not enforced like it should. If someone with bad intentions really wanted to get on base they could. I entered and exited four times and never questioned, and yet they wonder why shit happens. If people did their job there would not be so many fatal incidents.

2
July

Saturday July 2, 2005

Victoria has an unexplainable way of making my day. I really enjoyed talking to her yesterday morning. We have an agreement that by the time we both turn twenty four and have not found our soul mates, we will get married. I will be twenty three in over a month. That day is not to far away, whether or not that will happen I do no not know. I would really like for it to happen. I genuinely care and love her, she makes me happy. I think she was the reason why me and Ali did not make it. I just can't get her off my mind. We have been friends for over six years now. I've known her practically all my life. We have our fights, but we always get over it and forgive each other. I think the longest time we have been without talking to each other was a little over two months. I think we will always be in each others life. I am incredibly lucky to have a friend like Victoria. Who ever I end up with has to accept the fact that she will always be in my life.

Apache, was the bar we went to last night. I wasn't in the mood for drinking, but peer pressure is a bitch. The bar is located down town, Korea is so lighted at night. The evening was illuminated by different signs which were all different colors. Lights everywhere, it somewhat resembled New York city. The entrance to the bar was down a flight of stairs. The inside was extremely small. There were two female bar tenders by the names of Lime and Kelly. Koreans don't have those types of names. I'm assuming the names were for the Americans, to facilitate us in addressing them. Lime is very attractive, and I'm usually not attracted to Korean chicks. This girl is cute. She was very friendly, and conversed with us for a while. The other two guys I went with already knew her. As soon as we got there she played latin music for us, that was very nice of her. We also got into a conversation about her not liking white men. Apparently she is into black men, bummer.

I really did not want to get drunk, but I did. I wish I could quit completely, but I can't. I am very easily convinced into drinking. The fact that the drinks are so expensive should be enough reason to make me want to quit. Our tab was almost two hundred dollars, and there were only three of us. Other guys from our company showed up, including two sergeants. They were really cool. They had their own tab.

Lime set up a game of Jenga for us, the looser had to take a drink. This drink is called "Oh my God." I was the looser, but the other two guys ordered a drink for themselves as well. This drink was insane. It was in a beer glass, and they poured a variety of liquors into the glass. Once they were done pouring liquor into the glass, it was filled with beer. On top of the glass they placed two straws. They set a shot glass on top of the straws. Once again they poured who knows what in the shot glass. They ignited the shots with a lighter. Lime placed a shot in her hand, dipped her finger in the shot, and then poured the shot in her mouth. She dipped her finger, she had previously placed in the shot, in the flaming shot on top of the glass. Now her finger was on fire. She placed the finger right in front of the three glasses and spat the liquor that was in her mouth. This caused a huge explosion. The fire caused the straws to melt. Once they melted the shot dropped into the glass, and immediately we chugged the drink. The explosion was huge, we had to move out the way, it was a really interesting sight. That drink will literally make you say "oh my God," several times. They took quite a while preparing the drinks. I think they did it on purpose, to build anticipation. I must admit, I was a bit nervous. It was surprisingly good, I was expecting it to taste awful. Well that drink got me drunk, after that I only had one beer. I was done.

This morning I woke up at about seven-thirty. I had to get ready to go to class. Luckily I did not wake up with a hang over, which surprised me because I mixed liquor with beer. I singed up for a stock market class through the University of Maryland. The class will be today and tomorrow, and I will get one hour credit. The class is interesting, but it is very difficult to understand the instructor. He has a very strong Korean accent. I do not know anything about the stock market, so it is very educational. It is a good thing that the Army will pay for our schooling. The only thing I paid for was the book, it was only twelve dollars. That is not much for a book.

Sunday July 3, 2005

It rains every freaking day here. I hate it. I hate it immensely. Back in Big Lake it does not rain very often, so the times it did rain I enjoyed it. Rain is a novelty in Big Lake. I have always said that I like the rain. When it rains every day you tend to despise it. Having an umbrella is essential here. This morning while walking to school, Parsons and I were talking about how gay we felt using an umbrella. I felt like men were not supposed to use them. I guess that I'm under the impression that men have to tough it out, and get wet if we have to. Regardless of how the umbrella makes me feel, I will have to continue using it other wise I will be drenched the whole time.

Last night I got drunk again. Peer pressure always gets me. I'm a sucker for drinking. I am failing miserably at my attempt to quit drinking. Once I start drinking the cigarette automatically fixates to my mouth. I guess I am never going to quit smoking either. I always said I wasn't a quitter.

Monday July 4, 2005

I finally started working today. I am working the day shift, that is from five in the morning to five in the afternoon. Twelve hours seems forever. I work inside a bunker. It's about a five minute walk from the barracks. I woke up at four this morning to get ready. It was entirely to early. I no longer have a hard time sleeping, so I can actually get some sleep. I can sleep past eight hours with no problem. Only got six hours of sleep, so I had a hard time staying awake at work.

Work consisted of watching movies. We watched a total of four movies, the *Passion of the Christ* being the last one. Excellent movie. The first time I watched it I cried. I saw the movie in the theater with Victoria, we both were brought to tears, it's such an intense movie. I was afraid to watch it, because I thought I wouldn't be able to contain myself. I sure didn't want to cry in front of everyone there. I was able to keep my cool, and didn't cry. This movie puts everything into perspective. Makes me realize how much God did for me, and how ungrateful I am. He sent his only son to die for our sins and transgressions, yet I have failed to place Him first in my life. Why am I so ungrateful? He has done so much for me, and I can't even go to church to praise Him. All he wants is for us to follow Him, we have so much to gain and nothing to loose. Nothing that matters anyway. We still manage to turn our back to Him, but when we are in the hole we always expect Him to get us out of it. One day I will get it right, hopefully it wont be to late.

Today I was invited to go to the ville. The plan was to go clubbing and barhopping. I said no. I was finally able to say no without being suckered in. I am trying really hard to quit drinking. If I would of gone I would have definitely drank. I am very proud of myself. My mother was also a part of the reason why I refused to go. When I called her this morning she got onto me for spending to much money. She gets my bank statements, so she sees how much money I spend. Had I gone who knows how much money I would have spent. A beer is an arm and a leg. Watching the *Passion of the Christ* made me feel like I should do the right thing. I do not want His sacrifice to be in vain. If God sacrificed his son for my sins, I'm definitely going to try and show gratitude. I should definitely watch this movie more often.

Tuesday July 5, 2005

I feel miserable today, being here does not feel right. It really sucks. I feel like a prisoner. On the weekends we have to be back on post by one in the morning, and at midnight on weekdays. We cannot have personal vehicles, and I'm in a country far from home. Loneliness has overpowered me today. I really haven't clicked with anyone here. I don't consider anyone here friends, the only person I can consider a friend is Jordan. I can't hang out to pass the time, I have no desire to hang out with anyone here.

People who join the Army sacrifice a lot. I think my biggest sacrifice is being away from home. I like being away, but I like to be close enough to visit if I want to. My brothers Kevin and Victor are growing up, and I'm missing out on being a part of their life's. I've been away four years on and off. Here in Korea it will be a complete year before going home. My oldest brother was a kid when I graduated and left home. Now he is twelve almost thirteen. He is becoming a teenager, and I feel like I do not know who he is. I want to get to know my brothers, spend time with them, and watch them evolve into their person as they mature throughout the years.

I still have over three years left in the Army. Three years in which I will miss out on numerous family gatherings. I missed my sister's wedding. The most important day of her life, and I wasn't there. Sometimes I ask myself if being here is actually worth it. I'm also going to miss the birth of my first nephew or niece.

The Army is helping me become independent, I'm traveling, experiencing a plethora of different things, and its keeping me from everyone I love. There are soldiers dieing in Iraq. Fathers and mothers who will never see their kids grow up, never hold then in their arms, watch them take their first step, or even see their grandkids. Broken homes will be left, left to struggle and move on without an essential and necessary person in their lives. I am so lucky to have grown up with both parents, some kids wont have that blessing. There is also young people dieing. They are not even old enough to drink, but old enough to die for this country. Dieing at twenty you don't even begging to experience life. Who is to say that I wont be sent to Iraq and become a casualty. There is a lot to loose by joining the Army.

I also think that when people make sacrifices, there is always something out there for us that will make everything worth it. I have faith that by having joined the Army I will accomplish many things and make my family proud.

I think that all these emotions I have today are because I'm feeling homesick. I actually miss my family today. I even put some pictures up where I could see them daily. I will be okay tomorrow.

Our room has been inspected twice today. Apparently my roommate is known for being dirty and unorganized. To make sure he is not living in a pigs pen, we have inspections on a regular basis. Since I've been here he has only helped me clean once, I would say they have a reason for checking up on him. It makes me feel like I'm dirty too. That is not the case at all. It is really annoying that they come in here to check our cleanliness. It makes me feel like I'm being checked up on as well. I am a grown man, I do not need to be monitored like a little kid. My roommate on the other hand is always been told what to do, I would be extremely fed up with that shit by now. It does take him a while before doing what he is supposed to, it takes him a couple of reminders.

Today I went and bought power bars, I am constantly skipping meals. Skipping meals is unhealthy, I don't like walking to the dinning facility, and ordering food is getting expensive. I was warned by my mother about spending to much money. Instead of skipping a meal I will have a power bar. They have all the vitamins and protein my body needs to get through the day. I also bought tuna, I was craving it with crackers and lime. It is very delicious. I also was craving cottage cheese and Doritos. I satisfied all my cravings today.

One of the sergeants just came in and told us that there is a possibility of an alert tomorrow. That really chaps my ass, and I'm all out of chap stick. Alerts are retarded and a half. I know it's for combat readiness, but it is really a joke. I hate doing stupid bullshit, in a real attack we would all be dead anyway. There is no plan, we just stand out there and wait. I am going to have to go to sleep early now. That blows, and tomorrow is my day off. A perfect way to ruin it.

Wednesday July 6, 2005

I was right, I'm over feeling nostalgic. I received and email from Victoria, that was enough to brighten my day. She has so much control over me, it's ridiculous, and we are merely friends. When you care for someone so much anything they do makes you happy. It is always the small things that count, by telling me she loves me and misses me is enough. Our friendship has really strengthen throughout the years.

The alert was not called, good, because I did not want to wake up early. This day has been a bum day, all I've done is lounged around and watch television all day. Tonight I will have to shine my boots, they are really particular when it comes to having shiny boots. Our uniforms have to always be pressed and our boots *blinging*. The KATUSA soldiers always out shine everyone else with their boots, I think they are required to spend an hour a day shining their boots. Not me, all I spend shining my boots is about ten minutes. The boots I have do not shine well, I will have to buy some better ones when I get my clothing allowance in October. After being a year in the Army we get extra money to buy any necessaries items that we might need. Like boots, uniforms, or running shoes. The first year the clothing allowance will only about a hundred and fifty bucks for me. My second year in the Army I will get more. We do not get that much money our first year, because everything that was issued to us should still be in good condition. After two years of wear something will tear, therefore; I will be getting more money next time around. The amount is also based on rank, the higher the rank the more money those soldiers will get.

Thursday July 7, 2005

Today I have been in Korea one month. So far so good, some days it really sucks, but some days I enjoy being here. Whatever happens I have to be here, so I got to suck it up. Like I have said before, I will make the best of it. I have eleven more months to go. Overall it has been decent. I only plan to stay here one year, any longer will be to long. There is other places that I need to see. I would really be keen on being back in the states for my next assignment. I miss my country.

Today the guy who was in the same company as me in AIT came to hang out and watch TV. His name is Nathan Hopkins. I had a couple of beers, he only had one, he doesn't like beer. Beer is definitely an acquired taste, there was a time long ago when I did not like beer.

We talked about why he joined the Army. Almost everyone who I've talked to once said that they would never join the Army, and almost everyone joined as a last resort. The Army does offer you opportunity, the opportunity to better ourselves, and the opportunity to do something completely out of our comfort zone. It is definitely a challenge, mentally and physically. More so mentally than physically.

Hopkins is very animated. I tell him he should be a comedian. He really has potential, this guy is funny.

We talked about our friends back home. For me my friends are in San Antonio, not in Big Lake. The roles that we played in our circle of friends. We looked back into our past, and talked about how different out life's have turned out.

Today two soldiers came to our room to document the serial number on our refrigerator and microwave. I had no idea where the serial number was located, I automatically assumed it was in the rear. I struggled to get the refrigerator from its place, to be able to see the back of it. Once I got it out of its place and looked behind it, there was a dead mouse. It had been there quite a while, because it was skin and bones. Goes to show how often my roommate cleaned. There was also food, dust, dirt, everything you could think of was underneath that refrigerator, even feathers. There was nothing else to do but clean it all up.

Friday July 8, 2005

I normally wake up ten minutes before four to get ready for work. I try to be there fifteen minutes prior to my shift, which begins at five in the morning. In order to get a good night sleep, I try to go to bed around nine. It usually takes me a while before I fall asleep.

I must have been asleep thirty minutes, when I hear a knock on the door. I'm thinking that if I ignore it they will know I'm asleep and leave me alone. I was wrong, the knocking only got louder and louder. I finally got up to see who it was. It was Parsons who needed to use the buttons from my class A coat, apparently he lost his. The class A uniform is only used in ceremonial events, sometimes inspections, and at graduation. I got back into bed, extremely pissed off. Know it's going to take another thirty minutes to fall asleep. Fifteen minutes later, a knock on the door. Once a gain I get up to see who it is. This time it was a sergeant, who was looking for my room mate. He works the night shift so he wasn't here.

I was really angry, I am very anal when it comes to getting sleep. When my room mate was on day shift he would answer the door. Know I'm the only one in here, so I have to answer the door.

Work is extremely boring. All I do is sit there and watch TV. I also escort the Koreans, who work there, in and out of the building. They do not have security clearances; therefore, they are not allowed to enter or exit without an escort. They do the majority of the work, we just sit there. I think I might of answered the phone twice. The Koreans speak English, but is almost impossible to understand them. I always say "okay" or "really," when they tell me something. I don't ever know what the hell they're saying. Those two words usually does the trick.

Saturday July 9, 2005

Gabriel's feelings about Sheena have changed drastically. He got drunk and sent her a very rude email. Why do drunk people do that? I did the same thing with Victoria once, that was when we stopped talking. He says she hurt him, and he was tired of having to change who he was so she would like him. He went on and on, on how much he hates her now. Of course this took Sheena by surprise, I told her he would come back around, Gabriel can't play the evil guy for to long.

The reason why I think Gabriel is acting this way is because he is talking to someone else. He told me that while he was home he got back in touch with an old flame. He was engaged to this girl at one point This girl, according to him is everything he looks for. It's not so much Sheena hurt him, I think it's his way of saying I'm done with you, I've found someone else. Now he is looking for any excuse to cut Sheena off.

Monday July 11, 2005

I despise when people are not punctual! We were supposed to meet at the company at ten till five, this morning. We were to depart to Yong Song, for drivers training, no later than fifteen after five. We left ten after six. The sergeants always do this, and it pisses me off. I could have slept till five in the morning, instead of getting up at ten till four. That's part of the Army "hurry up and wait." During basic training we had to wait for everything. Going to chow even required waiting. I should be used to it by now.

Drivers training was extremely boring. We watched several videos, and they put me to sleep. Our instructor had to walk out for a while, and that was when I knocked the fuck out. I will have a whole five days of training. That means I will be away from the company, and be able to sleep more. Instead of getting up ten till four, I will be getting up at six-thirty. That is definitely a plus. One can never get to much sleep.

Our instructor is Korean, I have a hard time understanding him. At the beginning of the class he gave a lecture on driving in Korea. I probably understood about forty percent of what he said. If I do not pass I will blame it on him.

I found a pubic hair in my mouth! How it got there I do not know. This room we are staying in is so fucking nasty. Nasty is an understatement, it's obscene. The furniture is all broken. The mattress is old, dirty, full of stains, and smells. Good thing we got clean sheets, and a mattress pad. I do not want to have to lay in a cum stained mattress. I think my sheets were new, because they had stickers with a bar code on them. The rug here is disgusting, it's full of crumbs, pubic hair, and toenails everywhere. The chairs are covered in stains. Instead of being maroon, they are black. The pubes are scattered throughout the room. Someone must of trimmed their bush in here, and didn't clean up after themselves.

Tuesday July 12, 2005

Eva Mendes, will star in the comedy *The Wendell Baker Story* with Luke and Owen Wilson. I auditioned for this movie in Austin, Texas. My friends Eric and Amber went with me. We got lost several times before we found the address. Map Quest does not always give clear directions. It is somewhat upsetting to hear this, because I could have met Eva Mendes. That would have been awesome, and the fact that would have been my first movie. It sucks that I didn't get that part. I don't even remember the characters name, I auditioned for. It has been a while back.

When I was called to audition, I was in Big Lake, which is about almost five hours away from Austin. It all happened at a very short notice. I was told one day prior to the audition, so I left to San Antonio that same day. I printed the script at Eric's grandmothers house. The script I was emailed was only two pages, and three lines of dialogue for my character. The script said nothing about my character, so I couldn't place myself in his shoes. I had no idea what they were looking for, and no clue as to what my character was like. I think that if I would have had a description of what my character was like, I would have prepared for it and played the part better.

I think it was in the summer of 2003 when I auditioned, and almost two years later I hear about who will star in the movie. I knew that the movie was going to be produced or written by Luke and Owen. I'm not sure how involved they were, but I knew it was there project. I had no idea that they would be starring in the movie as well.

I'm such a looser! If I would of gotten that part I would not be here today. It's so odd that something can completely turn your life the opposite direction. Everything happens for a reason. I know that's the biggest cliché, but it's so true. I hope that movie does well.

I also auditioned for *The Assistant* with Andy Dick. When I was auditioning, I did not know it was to be his assistant. I'm glad I didn't go on that show. Andy Dick is a freak.

Its news like this that put me in a bad mood. They make me realize how much my life sucks. I really suck at life. The more I look at things the more I realize that the Army is not for me. Eric always told me that joining the Army was completely out of character for me. He tried to convince me not to do it, but I had ran out of options. I did not want to live a boring life in Big Lake. Somehow I find myself being bored here to.

At least I am doing something not everyone is brave enough to do. Not everyone is brave enough to join the Army at a time of war. Someone has got to defend this country; therefore, allowing everyone else to enjoy their freedoms and life in America. Hundreds are out there dieing, someone has got to replace them. The ones who are not dead need a brake, a brake to come back and see their families. Someone has got to relieve them. Not everyone can be a movie star. We all have different callings. We all have a role to play in this chaotic world we live in. I am still figuring out what role I'm to play, right now my role is to be a soldier. And I will do it to the best of my ability.

I read an interesting quote by Kelly Osbourne, in *Blender* magazine. When asked, who do you think you are. She responded, "I have no fucking idea. I have so many questions about myself, how I look at things, how I should say things. What I want to do with my life…and when you know who you are, you don't have to ask yourself those questions." That is so true, part of life is figuring out who we are and what makes us do what we do. Once we figure that out, what is left to do. We spend all of our life searching for answers, answer we may never get.

Thursday July 14, 2005

I waited an hour and a half in the blistering heat. I sat under the shade of a tree as sweat rolled down parts of my body it had never rolled before. My ass went sore, then numb from sitting on the hard asphalt. Lucky for me I had a bottle of water, otherwise I would of dehydrated. I also entertained myself by reading *Maxim*, a great men's magazine.

Finally, I see the HMMWV pull up, and get myself mentally ready to drive. The first thing out of the sergeant's mouth was "where is your cell phone."

"Its in my room," I responded.

He said he tried to call me, to tell me that I was not going to be driving. That way I wouldn't have to wait, for me just to go to my room. They knew my cell phone does not work. That is why I have kept it in my room the whole time we've been here.

When I got to my room, I checked my cell phone. There was a missed call. Apparently my cell phone receives calls, but I cannot dial out. He called at 2:58pm, and I saw him about five minutes later. What a difference that would have made. I think he changed his mind about me driving, right at the last moment. I didn't get mad, because Parsons did the waiting yesterday. It was my turn to wait.

Speaking about Parsons, I am such an asshole to this guy. Today I actually apologized, because I caught myself being an asshole. Then I realized I had been an asshole all week. I get so much humor out of being rude. It keeps me going. In AIT I made fun of Gabriel, he was such an easy target. The fact that he took everything personal made it even more amusing. Until the day he cursed at me, and denied me as his friend. I had to tone down the asshole in me. It seems like the asshole is back, because here lately I've been on a role. I told Parsons since Gabriel was gone, now it was his turn to be picked on.

Being rude is exceedingly comical, it makes me ecstatic. I get a kick out of it. I think being rude and sarcastic runs in the family. My sister Christina, is the queen of rudeness. My aunts and uncles are all very sarcastic. Even my grandmother puts her two sense in, every know and then. I do not do it out of malice, because I'm only rude to people I know and like. Most of the time I don't perceive it as being rude. The majority of the time I'm being honest. I will say what people only think in their minds.

Friday July 15, 2005

I am officially licensed to drive in Korea. I desperately hope I never have to drive here. People here do not know how to drive. I would probably get lost as well.

Drivers training is over. My vacation is over, no more sleeping late, and getting off early. Back to dealing with everyone else, and waking up early. It was pleasant to be away from everyone else, at least for a week.

Saturday July 16, 2005

On Friday the company had an exercise, so today we have to clean up all the vehicles they dirtied. Here I was thinking Saturday I was going to be off. This really sucks because everyone who was in drivers training was not a part of the exercise, but we are a part of the recovery group. Recovery is a glorified word for clean up. Clean up after everyone else.

I hate the way the Army works. There is so much politics involved here. It is all one enormous political game. All about kissing the right ass, and being extremely fake to keep everyone happy. Thinking about dealing with the way things work here, makes me sick to my stomach.

The Army is a communist organization with in a democracy. It is all about power here. There is nothing a private like me can do, when a sergeant handles an incident with extremely poor judgment. Regardless of how wrong he may be, it does not matter. His rank automatically makes him right. The Army is going to drive me mad. I have always been very outspoken and forward, now I have to keep everything to myself and accept the nonsense. The repercussions for questioning someone's authority are way to severe. They will never admit how wrong they are. Even if it's so evident that everyone else sees it. I hate playing games, and unfortunately the Army is one big political game.

Sunday July 17, 2005

I'm a bitch! Being a private in the Army is basically being everyone's bitch. It is do this and do that, while the person giving the orders sits on his fat ass. Everyone has been through this, in the beginning if their military career. AIT was for the most part landscaping and janitorial work, my first duty station is being everyone's bitch. I wonder what will be next.

Last night I got drunk with Parsons and Hopkins. I went to bed about midnight and woke up late this morning. As I walked out the door to go to work, I thought to check up on Parsons. I knocked on his door several times, and no answer. His door was unlocked, so I went into his room. He was still asleep. I tried to wake him up, but he was knocked out. I even poured water on him and it didn't work. I had to shake him abruptly, and he finally woke up. His alarm didn't go off. I left to go to work and he stayed behind to get ready.

I was not late I arrived there right on time. I was immediately told to start pushing, for not being fifteen minutes early. I didn't even shave or shine my boots. I don't care at this point I'm feeling very lethargic. I'm also counting the days until my Army days are over.

Monday July 18, 2005

Parsons and I were on shift by ourselves today. The Korean civilians were there, but no military personnel was there. It was great, I loathe being watched all the time. It was advantageous for us, because we learned more in a day, than what we have the whole time we've been here. We did everything with help from the civilians, but for the most part it was us who did everything.

Work is usually dead, but today it wasn't. We had a couple of circuits that went out and a couple that were brought back in. For once the day went by faster than usual. Primarily because we actually did something. The first three hours of shift are designated for sleep. We wake up to early to be at work, so we have to have time to regain the sleep we are missing out on. Nothing happens the first three hours anyway.

I have a difficult time understanding what the Koreans tell me. Their accents are very strong. I guessed half the time at what they were saying, I simply nodded my head in agreement. One of the Koreans was explaining what I had to do. I had no clue what the hell he said. He also had very bad breath, so that kept from concentrating on what he was saying. Next time I will give him a Tic Tac.

Today my goal was to get as much sleep possible. Well that all changed when Hopkins came and knocked on my door and told me we would be drinking. I said, "sorry but I wont be drinking today." He wasn't having it, so Parsons, Hopkins, and I are currently drinking. I'm telling you peer pressure is a fucking bitch. I absolutely can't say no when it comes to drinking. Now my goal has changed to not getting completely wasted. Sleep is for the weak.

For years I have tried to get rid of my gut. I owe it all to my drinking. I hate having a beer belly. As long as I continue drinking my belly is not going anywhere. I have so many reasons to quit drinking and none of them have done the trick yet. I hope I don't end up an alcoholic. Drinking excessively runs in the family, I was destined to be a drinker. Maybe I will grow out of it. It is probably just a phase, I hope this phase don't last more than a decade.

Ali disliked the fact that I drank. That is how she met me and that's how I intended on staying. I lied constantly to her about not drinking. She refused to date someone who could potentially become an alcoholic. Lying was always easier than attempting to quit drinking. I feel so sorry for her. She is a wonderful person, she did not deserve running into an asshole like myself. Sometimes I regret being an asshole, so she could break up with me, but I wasn't planning on changing. We never had sex, she wanted to wait until she got married. I respect that, but I sure was not going to wait. That was another major reason why I did not try to salvage our relationship.

Wednesday July 20, 2005

"Second to None," can begin to sound like "suck on my nuts," when shouted at a fast speed. Today I was on force protection, which is basically standing by the back gate saluting incoming and exiting vehicles, while sounding off to our motto "Second to None." we also check identification cards as they enter the gate, the only time we did that was when the Korean gate guard was busy with someone else. She did the identification checks for the most part of our shift.

The weather was humid and hot, and with all of our gear on it seemed like it was twice as hot. I will be on force protection for the next six days. It's a total of eight hours a day broken down to two four hour shifts. One from ten to two in the afternoon, and the other from ten to two in the morning. The time does slowly progress, but I like being isolated from the company. I like to stay away from everyone else. I enjoy doing something with little or no supervision, not to mention sometimes I really don't like talking to anyone. Not being able to talk to anyone is why most soldiers despise doing it. That's actually what makes it more appealing to me. I do not like being fake and pretend that I enjoy talking to people when I don't, it actually annoys me. People who I really don't care to get to know. I can usually decide whether or not I will like someone within the first ten or fifteen minutes of meeting them.

I hate fake people, especially ass kissers. I will never kiss anyone's ass to get ahead. I've noticed how fake people can be and how much of an ass kisser they can become to get something, or simply to be liked. I really do not care to be liked. I used to care what people had to say about me and whether or not they liked me, but I figured out that the more I did that the less I liked myself. Parsons can sometimes kiss ass, but I overlook that because he has been my friend. He is also the biggest bullshitter I've met. It does irritate me though. I can become annoyed by people very frequently and easily. I wonder why I'm like that. That's why I rather be by myself.

I did however enjoy talking to the female security guard who was on force protection. She was attractive, that was probably the main reason conversing with her was so enjoyable. She wouldn't tell me her age, all she let me know was that she was older than twenty four. She thanked me for thinking she was that young. That leads me to believe that she could be quite older. She looked very young to me. Talking to Koreans is always pleasant, they don't put up a front. Americans for the most part, always put up a façade.

Thursday July 21, 2005

During my second shift of force protection yesterday, the security guard got in trouble for having a visitor, during working hours. It might have been her boyfriend, because they were very touchy feeling with each other. They were warned by a sergeant who happened to be walking in the gate, he told the guy he had to leave. The sergeant walked off, but kept watching from a distance. They guy did not leave, they both even witnessed that the sergeant was observing them. They both seemed not to care and continued talking as if they weren't told anything. Finally the sergeant came back, and took both of their information and reported them. Turns out that they guy she was talking to was a security guard. He probably assumed that it was alright for him to be there since he was a security guard.

After that whole incident nothing happened. I could not stay awake at all. I'm used to going to sleep early. I think I slept a hour and a half of my four hour shift.

It went by fast. When the next shift came to relieve us the security guard asked me out loud, "did you sleep well." One of the soldiers who was coming on shift was a sergeant, I thought she was going to tell me something. But she didn't.

Today we had a male security guard. I was looking forward to work with the female security guard, even though she called me out for sleeping. She probably did not want to be the only one to get in trouble. Once again the weather was very hot and humid. The soldiers who were to relieve us were late. I was pissed off. Twenty minutes seems like an eternity when I'm standing in the damned sunlight.

Friday July 22, 2005

Today I received an email from the girl I cheated on Ali with. I met her during AIT, and the last month and a half we were there we hooked up. I thought I was doing it just for fun. I told myself it didn't mean anything. She had someone else, and I had someone. I feel like a part of me still wishes we were seeing each other. She tells me she cares about me and thinks of me frequently. I brighten up her days when I send her emails. She wants to visit me during Christmas. She made me feel like no other girl has. She was really into me and I liked that. She is another reason why me and Ali did not work out. How am I supposed to know what to do. Even if I wanted to be with her its not going to happen, I'm in Korea and she is in the states with her boyfriend. I'm destined to be alone. I pray to God for that not to happen.

I talked to my dad today, he got a new job. It's not as physically demanding as his current job. He's not getting any younger, so I'm glad he was offered that job. The downfall to that is that he has to continue to work in New Mexico, so he will be away during the week. The only time he will be home will be on the weekends.

Saturday July 23, 2005

My force protection shift went by fairly fast this morning. Every shift I get the Koreans to help me learn their language. As soon as I'm off shift I forget everything I've learned. The Korean language is extremely complex. Everything sounds the same to me.

Today I took a nap, I wasn't even planning on sleeping. I was laying down and I passed out. Once I woke up I noticed I had slept three hours. I must have been extremely exhausted. Standing in the heat really beats up your body. It could be worse, I could be in the desert. It must be very hard being out there.

I feel lonely today. Usually Victoria's emails cheer me up, but not today. I have a weird feeling in my stomach. I feel empty inside. Maybe it's heat exhaustion, or might be the fact that I miss my home and family. A million things are going through my mind today. I should probably read the bible, that always seems to work. If I were more sociable I wouldn't feel so lonely, but I really don't care to get to know anyone here. I will be fine tomorrow I always get over it by the next day.

While in AIT, I don't ever recall feeling lonely, but then again I called home almost everyday. I have always been very close to my family, and always kept in touch. Now that I'm here I can't call home every day, calling cards are too expensive. Other than my dad and my mom, and my sister and grandma on occasion, I don't keep in touch with anyone else.

I have always stayed in touch with my friends in San Antonio, and I have not called any of them since I've been here. In AIT I always talked to Nikki, she always made me laugh. I have not called her in over a month. Nikki always helps to make any situation feel less trivial. We always talk about stupid crap. I should call her, I could use a good laugh. Gabriel always calls, and he has not called in a while. I get a kick out of talking to him.

Life really sucks today! Might as well drink bleach.

I will have to buy a calling card tomorrow, I need to call people up. I need to hear familiar voices.

I was looking at the pictures I have of my family, and I got teary eyed. I really miss them, a lot of them I only saw for a couple of minutes. I did not manage my time well while I was home. Fifteen days is not enough time to see everyone. I have a very big family.

I know Mama Blanca and Papa Beto, feel like I have neglected them. I do not call them enough, and only visited them once while I was home. Mama Blanca and Papa Beto are my grandparents on my mother's side of the family. I love them to death, they mean the word to me, I need to start showing them that. My other grandparents live next door to me, it requires no effort on my part to see them. That's usually my first stop after I would wake up in the mornings. Breakfast was always there and sometimes lunch and dinner.

Sunday June 24, 2005

I'm over feeling lonely, it never lasts more than a day. I did buy a calling card, I'll call home during force protection tonight. I talked to Gabriel already, he's doing good. He is currently training for a triathlon. Gabriel is a great athlete, more than

I can say for myself. He finally sent Sheena an email and apologized. I new he would get over it and over her.

I also got to talk to Amber and Eric. They were upset because I didn't visit them while I was in San Antonio. I didn't even call them. I lied to them and told them I had to leave the next day, so I wasn't able to see them. I felt bad because they were looking forward to see me. I arrived in San Antonio on a Friday and left on Sunday. I didn't want to ditch my aunt either. I was really tired from the trip, so I didn't feel like going anywhere. Two and a half days was barely enough time to divide amongst my aunt, grandparents, and Victoria.

They are genuinely good friends, and very talented. Amber released a Spanish album when she was thirteen, and did very well for someone her age. Eric was one of her backup dancers, that's how they met. He later joined a boy band, that didn't quite work out for him though.

Once Amber has her baby she will go back to the studio and begin to work on her English album. She plans to name her baby Emperess Romance. I told her kids would make fun of her name, but she really likes that name. The name is unique, I suppose.

I bought a box of cigarettes. I was carving one really bad, and Parsons wasn't around for me to bum one off him. I have no will power. I wasn't able to finish the whole cigarette, I only smoked about half of it. Half was enough to satisfy my craving. Cigarette companies should consider making smaller cigarettes, for people who only smoke to satisfy a craving, and are trying to quit. I've tried putting it out and saving it for later, but the second time a cigarette is lit doesn't taste very well.

I have learned so much about the Korean culture, know that I've been on force protection. The Korean security guard was telling me that Korean women find foreigners attractive when they can speak their language. I'm going to have to learn Korean.

It is very offensive to them when American soldiers curse in Korean. She said that if we are going to curse, to curse in our own language. I think they feel it's directed at them, what other reason who someone curse in a language that is not their own.

They also think we are very rude and loud. During the night shift a lot of the soldiers come in drunk, so of course they are gong to be loud, rude, and forget their manners. Soldiers will also not pay the cab drivers. They will tell the driver that they just have to go to the ATM and withdraw money, and will be back to pay them. The soldiers never come back.

Tattoos are very frowned upon by Koreans. To them tattoos make a person look like a criminal. Anyone who is tattooed is not allowed in pubic pools or saunas. I was joking with the security guard and told her she should get a tattoo. She said if she did she wouldn't be able to get married. Korean men do not like women with tattoos.

People here get married at a much older age. Usually around late twenties early thirties. First of all a woman will not marry a suitor, until he has served his two year term in the Army. He becomes a man only when he has completed his term in the Army. That is when they are respected by society and taken seriously by a woman.

Korean women also think it is disrespectful when a soldier tells her she is pretty or beautiful. They do not take that as a compliment. Compliments from strangers are offensive to them. Only when a friendship has been established is a comment like that permitted.

Monday July 25, 2005

It's incredible how talking to my family and friends can make me feel. I was extremely indifferent about being here, about life, and every thing in general. After talking to my friends, my aunts, and grandma I have a new outlook. They help me to stay positive. Having a strong relationship with my family has become essential to me. My success in the Army and life will be because of them. Above all God has brought me this far, and I thank him everyday for a wonderful family he has given me. Yes, we are very dysfunctional, and bicker amongst each other, and sometimes don't talk to each other, but at the end of the day I know they will always have my back. I will always have theirs.

I did not get to talk to Nikki. When I called her she answered the phone but could not hear me. I tried several times to call her and each time she was not able to hear me. I could hear everything that she would say. She would quickly hang up, she probably thought that some one was prank calling.

My aunt Nora was very thrilled and relieved to have talked to me. When I was home I only saw her for fifteen minutes. The fact that I'm going to be gone for a whole year had her torn. We are only eleven months apart, and grew up together. We are very close, she is like my sister. She had no idea when I had left, and the day she found out that I was gone, she cried all day. Till this day every time she sees a picture of me and there is a conversation about me she is brought to tears. She was glad that I called her.

Today was the start of Warrior Storm, a ten day exercise where being at war is simulated. During these ten days we are not allowed off post, except for emergencies only, we cannot consume tasty alcoholic beverages, and we are not allowed to wear civilian clothes. The exercise kicked of this morning with an alert. I did not have to participate in the alert, since I'm on force protection, all I had to do was sign in. After that I went back to sleep. The exercise is supposed to create a high stress level for us, to determine how well we can work under high paced stressful conditions. I see it as a way to save money. A whole week without spending money on alcohol or going off post. Warrior Strom is somewhat of a practice for our three week long exercise we will have in late August.

My biggest pet-peeve is when people are late. I despise with a passion having to wait, it drives me insane. I would much rather have a cigarette put out in my eyeball, than have to wait. I've been in the Army almost a whole year and I still have not become accustomed to waiting. It annoys me when soldiers are late, for the majority of the time the two soldiers who relieve us have been late. It hasn't been the same two soldiers either, but they are all from the same company. That whole company needs a class on being on time. If I can manage to always be fifteen minutes early so can anyone else. There is no excuse for being late. One should always schedule unexpected occurrences that will delay the arrival to our destination. When you do that, you will never be late. It is not fair to make someone wait solely because you are to lazy to leave a couple of minutes early. I hate people who always wait to the last minute to do shit.

Tuesday July 26, 2005

My blood boiled as it ran through my veins. My anger was at an ultimate climax. There was no way to release the wrath, other than by smoking. Smoking calms me down, and the acceleration of my heart pumping decreases with each puff. The temperature begins to cool, and my blood goes back to its original flow. We pulled an extra four hours of force protection, last night, which triggered my anxiety. One of the soldiers was not aware he was scheduled to be on force protection. He also lives off post, so no one was able to contact him. The other individual simply did not show up.

Right as my shift was ending I was overwhelmed with exhaustion. I was at the point where I could have fallen asleep standing up. When the clock kept ticking, and no one showed up, I got angry. The heat began to flow through my veins and gave me a staggering amount of energy. My exhaustion was but a fizzling state of mind. I was so infuriated, I thought I was going to burst out of my skin. The amount of anger and anxiety, seemed almost impossible to fit within me. Lucky for me the security guard had cigarettes, and I found myself calmed and accepting, of what ultimately filled me with rage.

With an extra four hours on my hands all I did was stare into space. I have noticed that since I've been here, I have yet to see any stars. Perhaps the excessive amount of lights creates a barrier between the stars and their visibility. It's not pollution, because the air is fairly clean.

The two soldiers who were missing in action pulled our shift this morning. It was only fair that they do so. I was able to catch up on my sleep and recuperate all the lost energy. Even though we just stand there, the heat makes it very exhausting. I am extremely glad that tonight will be my last shift and tomorrow will be my day off. That day off is very much deserved.

Wednesday July 27, 2005

Last night was my last night of force protection. It was somewhat of a bitter sweet moment. I enjoy talking to the Korean security guards. I learned a little more Korean while on force protection. Force protection was also a way to disassociate my self from everyone. I'm glad force protection is over because I hate having to wait for the late soldiers to come on shift. One of the two soldiers who didn't show up for their shift was a sergeant. Our last shift ended with them being late again. He said it was due to the fact that they had to pull an eight hour shift. He thought we owed him for doing our shift. That is bullshit, we don't owe him anything. It was only fair that they do our shift after we did theirs. Suck it up, drink water, and drive on sergeant.

Today was a very well deserved day off. I slept until my eyes began to hurt. I will have to get accustomed to a different schedule. Tomorrow I will begin working the night shift. We'll see how that goes.

I also went to the gym, I had a good workout. There is nothing better than working up a good sweat. There is several ways of doing that. I get more energy after working out. That is also not the only way to get energy after a good sweat. If you know what I mean, but I have not had it yet.

Watching *Extreme Makeover Home Edition* reminded me of something I've always said I wanted to do. Ty Pennington is an extremely generous person to say the least. That guy has a reserved spot in heaven, if going to heaven was based on good deeds. He turns people's lives around by giving them new homes. He makes a difference in deserving families. Watching him and his crew change people's lives makes me feel the urge to do the same. I always said that I wanted to do something where I could make a difference.

I am making a difference by taking on the challenge of serving my country, a country that has given my family the opportunity to succeed and a chance to have a better life. I'm making a difference by doing something that many don't have the heart, bravery, or pride to do.

I get so caught up in the negative and not so comfortable side of the Army that I loose all perspective. We are ultimately here for a greater cause, and I support that cause. That's why I am here. Yes, this was last resort, but I believe in what I'm doing. I am extremely proud of the decision I've made to be here. I'm making a difference, not in one person's life but in a whole nation. The Army makes a difference and has allowed us to enjoy many freedoms other countries do not have.

God bless Ty, what he and his crew do is extremely honorable. There needs to be more people like him. People who care about others and their well being. We as a society are so self indulged in our own needs and wants that we do not see that there are people less fortunate, who could use our help. He is someone to look up to and a good role model.

Friday July 29, 2005

My first night shift was actually busy, since we are still in Warrior Storm exercise a lot is going on at work. I'm using equipment I had never used, so the exercise is a good way to get acquainted with all of our equipment. I was hoping to be able to sleep, but that did not happen. The twelve hours did go by fast however.

Working this shift screwed up my sleep. I got a little over three hours of sleep. My phone kept ringing. I ignored it and didn't answer the phone, but they came and knocked on my door and asked me to call in to work. They are asking me questions about the problems we had last night. How am I supposed to get any sleep if they keep bugging me. Even if I wanted to sleep I cant, once I get up I have a hard time falling back to sleep.

I am very tired and don't feel like conducting physical training today. Working the night shift is going to take a while to get used to. I need to purchase some Benadryl to pass out, that usually does the trick. I have to work out more often, because I have a PT test on August ninth. I want to get a good score, but today I don't feel like working out.

They couldn't find my weapon yesterday. The day I started force protection I was told to leave my weapon in the force protection arms room, someone from our company would go get it from there. They forgot all about it, and tried to blame me. When a private is not at fault, they will find a way to cast the blame on us.

Saturday July 30th 2005

I feel so incompetent when I don't know what is going on. There is a shit load of things going on at work, and I am clueless as to what is happening and how to fix it. What consoles me is the fact that no one else knows what the problems are and how to fix them. They only pretend to know what is going on, but the problems remain unfixed. If they knew what was going on they would be able to fix it. Every day at work feels like being on the job for the first day. That first day on the job everything is foreign and overwhelming. That is exactly how I feel when I go to work. When I think I have figured it out something else comes up and ruins my understanding. It is very chaotic I am ready for this exercise to be over. That way I can go back to watching television and answering the phone, that's always much easier.

Victoria is torn between two guys. That seems to always be the problem with her. Her life is very dramatic, and not the least bit boring. I do not know what exactly she is looking for, but I hope she finds it.

My sister told me she loved me and to take care. I wish she would stay pregnant longer. She is so much nicer know, I knew she had it in her. It could also be the fact that she wants me to buy her a new Dooney & Bourke purse. I always wondered what triggered her to be so rude. Doctors always go back to child hood for everything. Everything stems from childhood they say. We had a good childhood for the most part. She got away with everything, being the only girl made her blameless. I don't believe every malfunction or characteristic trait starts at childhood, some things we pick up as we go through life. I am very pleased to know she has a heart. I could have sworn she had a stone instead, and that cement ran through her veins.

Sunday July 31, 2005

The night shift is awesome, it is the most gratification I've had since I've been here. It started out rough but it's great know. I get to sleep, watch TV, and eat. Very view phone calls come in at night, so I don't even answer the phone all that much. Rarely do I have to get up from my chair. There is a lot of people who come in and out because of the exercise. They all leave at about eleven o'clock. That's when the lounging begins. Once this is over they won't come in at all.

Gabriel is getting married. He will be getting married to his high school sweetheart. They were engaged once but called it off. They are now picking up where they left off and getting married. I hope he knows what he is getting himself into. He did ask me not to tell Sheena, I wonder why.

3

August

Tuesday August 2, 2005

As much as I try to stay positive and motivated, is not happening. Going to work stresses and frustrates me. Primarily because I feel so useless. I finally understand what is going on, but everyone wants answers as to how to solve the problem. I barely know what is going on, much less how to provide a solution. I feel worthless. Part of this exercise was to create a stressful work environment, and that has been accomplished.

Wednesday will be the final day of the exercise, thank God, but on the fifteen we start another exercise. UFL will last a total of three weeks. I'm ready to get it over with. The month of August is going to suck balls. That's another tree weeks of no drinking, every one is going to go mad.

I should have picked a different MOS. My MOS, which is Network Switchboard Operator/Maintainer is very technical. I'm not a technical person. I barely know how to operate the basic functions of a computer, but this was the only MOS that seemed somewhat interesting. I also picked this MOS because they told me I would be working in an air conditioned facility. That suckered me in. Everything else I got offered was a combative MOS, I did not want that. I was not ready to go strait to the grave yet.

Every MOS I was interested in was reserved for students. Students who were coming strait out of high school, they have priority. I should have joined then, but at that time the Army never crossed my mind. I even missed school the day we took the ASVAB, that's how sure I was that joining the Army was not an option. If I enjoyed what I was doing it would be so much different. All this technical shit turns me off. If you plan on joining the Army do it right out of high school, you have the priority for the better jobs. Make sure you know exactly what your job will be.

During AIT I always remained positive. Throughout the four and a half months I was there, numerous soldiers tried to take their lives. Having a soldier on suicide watch was very frequent, to the point where we thought nothing of it. AIT was hard for some, but I enjoyed it and always managed to stay positive. The drill sergeants couldn't even bring me down, I was determined to make it trough. AIT was a learning environment, here we are expected to know what to do. About twenty percent of what we learned, is what we actually do here. The other eighty percent is all new to me. I am determined to make it through being here, but my positive outlook was misplaced somewhere.

Hopkins has really caught on, he provides solutions to the problems we have. He has only been here about a month longer than Parsons and I. They look at Hopkins, and when they look at me, I'm sure they question why I'm not as pro-active as he is. Hopkins learns very quickly. I learn at a slower pace, and the fact that I do not like what I'm doing slows my learning process even further.

Wednesday August 3, 2005

Our shift last night was awesome, everything seems to have been solved. The captain did not show up, and the lieutenant stayed off or backs. Those two add an incredible amount of stress to the work environment. They make me feel like I'm being monitored. I abhor that feeling, in which every action is being scrutinized. They don't solve anything, I don't know why they are there, especially the captain.

Our captain is somewhat arrogant, I get a negative vibe from him. He doesn't strike me as someone who is easy to talk to. In one occasion I was giving him some information about what was going on, and he ignored me. I have no respect for people who cannot acknowledge someone who is speaking to them. I have to respect his rank, but not him as a person. Just because you are the captain doesn't make you a better person than me. Very typical for someone, to let a little bit of power get to their head, in the military.

The lieutenant on the other hand is a very friendly, accessible guy, but some of the stuff he makes us do is very questionable. Makes me wonder if he even knows what he is doing. Nobody really likes him, they say he gets on their nerves. He has still not gotten on my nerves, yet that is. He is very helpful though, he will go out of his way to help us.

Thursday August 4, 2005

Everyone is drinking, and getting their party on. Now that the exercise is over everyone is indulging in what we were depraved of. I'm not taking part in the drinking, as much as I would like to, I can't. I have to get up early tomorrow to go to work. Back to the morning shift, just as I was becoming accustomed to the night shift. I also do not want to drink until after my PT test. Smoking however I have not stopped doing. I smoke one cigarette a day, right after eating lunch. I figure one cigarette can't harm anything. It helps settle my food.

Last night at work me and Parsons we given a detailed description of all our equipment by our shift supervisor. It was very helpful, everything makes more sense now. This sergeant is an excellent NCO (Non Commissioned Officer), to bad he will be leaving in about a month. It is so much easier when someone takes the time to explain things, instead of expecting us to know everything that are obviously foreign to us.

I slept twelve hours today, it was great.

Saturday August 6, 2005

Yesterday, myself, Parsons, and a KATUSA soldier went to a Korean restaurant. As a Mexican I thought I had tasted spicy food, boy was I wrong. We ordered spicy chicken, this chicken was not spicy, it was flaming. It was so hot that even my ears were throbbing. I began to sweat and my nose began to run. The chicken was so hot, I had to order something else. I ordered mild chicken. The chicken was still very hot, but I could actually eat it without having to drink water after each bite. We ran through many pitchers of water. The chicken was so delicious that the spiciness did not matter. This morning however I paid the ultimate price for eating the chicken. Lets just say that my mouth and my lips were not the only part of my body that was on fire.

At this restaurant I had Soju for the first time. Soju is the Korean version of vodka. Nothing could have prepared me for that first shot. It was like taking a shot of rubbing alcohol. I don't like drinking rubbing alcohol. I only had two shots, Soju was not good at all. We didn't even finish the bottle, and the bottle wasn't very big. I think I will stick to beer.

After we got done eating we went to Apache. There we met up with two other soldiers. This was my third time at this bar, and it was the first time I saw locals there. The bar is usually filled with American soldiers. This time there were females there, it's usually male soldiers and their wife's. These were single Korean women.

I initiated a conversation with on of the girls, she spoke very little English. Somehow we managed to maintain a conversation. She was a very nice girl. The language barrier was a problem. I'm sure half of the stuff I said didn't make sense to her. She was there with a group of friends, who helped her out with English words when she couldn't think of them. They were all very good looking. I am becoming more fond of Korean women. She kept giving me a Korean snack. It looked like chips, but it was dried fish. It wasn't very appetizing, but the beer helped me swallow them.

After we left the bar we went to a club. The club was in a tall building, but the club was underground. Seems like everything is underground. We were the only ones there. It was a very different atmosphere. We had a waiter, I had never seen waiters at a club. He brought us two platters filled with different kinds of fruits, with the drinks we ordered. We had beer, but he opened the beer and poured it into the glass. They never do that at a club in the states, not in any of the clubs I've been to anyway.

After a while people began to show up. I had a good time. I hadn't danced in a while, I got a good workout there. The DJ played American music. He played slow songs, that wasn't cool. You don't play a slow song at a club, especially right after a really good song. It ruins the mood.

We were going to stay there past curfew. They said that it gets better around one in the morning, and we left at midnight. I really did not want to risk getting caught. Curfew violations are an automatic field grade Article 15. An Article 15 is a form of non judicial punishment. Soldiers loose their rank when given an Article 15, and they get assigned extra duties. The loss of rank means loss of money. I sure as hell do not want to loose any money. It really sucks here sometimes, I don't want to make it suck more by getting in trouble.

This morning I woke up with a hangover. I brushed my teeth, drank some water, and passed out again. I didn't get up until two in the afternoon. I usually do not get hangovers, but this time my head felt like it was going to explode. I did go ten days without drinking, so I do not feel bad for getting drunk. I earned this hangover. Hopefully this will not hinder my performance on my PT test.

The bathrooms here are shared between two rooms. There is two doors in the bathroom, each door leads to a different room. There is only one person in the other room and my roommate and I in the other. A total of three people use the bathroom. Since I've been here, I have been the only one who has cleaned the bathroom. I will purposely not clean the bathroom, to see if the other two will clean it. It never gets done. That explains why when I got here the bathtub was brown, instead of its original color which is white. The shower curtain was black on some parts, and covered with residue. Needles to say, I purchased a new shower curtain. The toilet was many other colors besides white. I hate it that they don't do their part, but I'm not going to leave it dirty until they decide to clean the bathroom. I rather do it myself. After I'm done my roommate will say it was the other guys turn to clean the bathroom, but it's never his turn. So today I spent my evening wiping piss and pubes off the toilet. I talked to my dad while cleaning the bathroom, so I did not think to much on what I was doing. I just did it.

Sunday August 7, 2005

Today was my last day of working out before the PT test. Monday I will rest, and drink as much water to be properly hydrated for the PT test on Tuesday. My work out did not go very well, I had to stop half way through. I was running out of breath and energy. I don't know if I was running out of breath because of the drinking and smoking on Friday, or because I had only eaten a muffin all day long before working out. Hopefully this will not happen on Tuesday. I had told myself that I would not drink until after my PT test, so much for that.

I wasn't going to let my lack of energy keep me from working out. I stopped running briefly. Once I caught my breath I started running again. I did a thirty minute workout on the tread mill, lifted weights, and worked on my sit ups. I know I will pass my PT test, but I want to get a good score. What sucks is that I will be doing it on my day off. I will have to get up early because the PT test starts at six in the morning.

Monday August 8, 2005

I called my aunt this morning to see how Steven was doing. According to her, he is doing good, and will be graduating basic training on August 31st. He did get in trouble for fighting. I think it wasn't that big of a deal, because he wasn't counseled. That's good, you don't want to come out of basic training with an Article 15.

Getting along with everyone in a platoon is impossible. For two and a half months you live and share space with complete strangers. Everyone has different personalities, and eventually are bound to clash. People start getting on your nerves, and you are forced to live and train with them on an everyday basis. Arguments were an everyday occurrence during basic training. There were a couple of instances were fights almost broke out, but there was always some there to stop them. Having to live with people you don't know, and to deal with them becomes stressful.

The appointed leadership always took their position to serious, they became drill privates. There was always arguments with the platoon guide, no one likes taking orders from another private. We went trough four platoon guides during basic training. Our last platoon guide was the worse. He would assign the fire guard roster to his convenience. I found my self pulling fire guard or CQ several times a week. During fire guard we had to clean the bathroom, sweep and mop the floor. The first shift usually did the cleaning, during the two hours of shift I would write letters. We also had to make sure that everyone was in bed and not doing anything that they weren't suppose to. During CQ we would sit in the drill sergeants office and answer the phone. The first shift would clean the office. Sometimes they would make us sweep out side. I actually liked doing CQ, because I was able to wash my clothes. We would turn in our laundry twice a week, but we would still wash in between. We dirtied a lot of clothes training. We were issued view uniforms, therefore; we were constantly washing them. Two people were on shift at all times. At most he would do one or two shifts a week, and the platoon guide was always on the first shift. The first shift was always the best to do, because it didn't mess up our sleep time.

I hated that guy! He always had buggers running down his nose. He would rarely wipe them, only after someone told him he had a bugger. How could he not know he had buggers. They almost drained into his mouth. Very view people in our platoon liked him. Every one who liked him was everyone I did not like.

There is an award that they give at graduation, to the best soldier of the cycle. Our platoon guide received that award. They picked him out of the whole company. He didn't deserve that. About a week before graduation he got caught steeling. He and another couple of guys got caught steeling MREs (Meals Ready to Eat). We would eat MREs when we were out in the field training, and could not make it back to the dinning facility. The food was not very tasty. The food in the MREs have been packaged for God knows how long. What everyone liked about them was that they came with candy. That was the only time that we were allowed to eat candy. They received no punishment, and he still received the award for best soldier of the cycle. That was a joke.

He was a good ass kisser, they always get ahead. What pisses me off the most is not the ass kisser, but the person who is being manipulated by the ass kissing. Do they not see that they are only being treated that way because someone has an ulterior motive. What dumb asses, because the ass kisser usually gets what he or she wants. One day it will catch up to them.

During basic training we are also assigned a battle buddy. The purpose is to become accustomed to the battle buddy system. It's a watch my back, I'll watch your back system. I was assigned to Castellanos. Castellanos had been in the states a couple of months before joining the Army. He came from El Salvador, he spoke very little English. At least that's what he made everyone think. Since I was the only other Spanish speaking individual, I got stuck with him. I had to translate what he didn't understand. I would get in trouble for talking, when I was actually translating. While I was translating I would miss what was being said at the time. If I waited till the end of a class, I would forget what was said. Either way I was fucked.

I don't know why but I didn't like him. At least that's what I thought, because if someone talked down on him for not knowing what to do, it would piss me off. I felt like I was the only one who had the right to be rude to him. I dealt with him on a everyday basis. Others would deal with him for a while and then they would always call me.

I think I disliked him because he got me in trouble. My plan during basic training was to stay under the radar. I wanted to do what I had to, but not get noticed. It didn't work out that way.

The way it works in basic training if your battle buddy gets in trouble, you take the punishment along with him. I found my self doing a lot of extra push ups. It wasn't the extra push ups that made me mad, it was the fact it made me feel like a screw up. When the drill sergeants know who you are they tend to keep a closer eye on you. If you never say anything and don't get in trouble they don't mess with you. It was impossible to stay under the radar with Castellanos.

What annoyed me the most was that he could have long conversations in English with everyone in the barracks, but when a drill sergeant told him something he never understood. When I would tell him he couldn't do this or that, he always did the opposite. It got to the point where I stop translating for him. If he was going to do what he wanted, then he didn't need me.

I always tried to find a way to get back at him. The day we did the gas chamber was a perfect day to get back at him. We were given the instructions on what to do once we got inside the gas chamber. We were to take our mask off and say our name, social security number, rank, and platoon name. Something like that, I don't remember exactly. Castellanos asked what we had to do. I told him he had to take his mask off when approached by the drill sergeant, and sound off with the information they wanted. I purposely left out rank. I didn't tell him he had to say his rank, that way he would mess up and have to stay in the gas chamber longer than the appropriate time. I wanted him to completely choke in the gas chamber, and have a utterly awful experience.

Karma is a bitch, and what goes around comes around. I didn't go inside the gas chamber with Castellanos, but he did fine. I don't know if he said everything, or left his rank out and was let go because of his language barrier. I really don't know. What did happen was that I forgot to say my rank. What I wanted him to forget, I forgot. I had an awful experience in the gas chamber, I had to do it twice. At that time I didn't know what I was forgetting, until the second time around. The drill sergeant told me exactly what to say. That first time I thought I was being picked on. I ran out of there, because it was so unbearable. They tried to hold me in, but after struggling with me they let me go. Once I came out I had to immediately go back in. After that day, I made a conscious effort to be nice to him. It didn't last to long though, I'm not very patient.

I was really rude to him, sometimes I would catch myself and I would apologize. I would occasionally feel sorry for him. He was in a different country. His wife and daughter were in El Salvador. He still had not even met his daughter. It was hard for him. Even though I was rude he still confided in me, and I was there to listen. I was the only one he could talk to about his personal issues. What ever happened during training, I left it there. At the end of the day I would calm down and my annoyance with him was gone for that day.

I'm not very nice to begin with. I would get aggravated by having to baby sit him in a sense. Every where he went I had to go. I was there to train not to baby sit anyone. At the end of it all I was glad he was my battle buddy. I learned a lot for him. Sometimes you are going to have to deal with and work with people who annoy you. I learned to look past that and do what ever had to get done.

Tuesday August 9, 2005

I tossed and turned all night. I also got up every hour to piss. I drank gallons of water, so I could be very well hydrated today. Every time I have something important to do the next day, I can never sleep. I get nervous and the nervousness keeps me awake. As much as I tried to fall asleep I couldn't.

It was raining when I went outside to formation. My guess was that they were going to cancel the PT test. I was correct. We will be taking the PT test tomorrow instead. I was disappointed, because I was ready to get it over with. My stomach was feeling a little weird so I'm glad that we didn't. That might of affected my sit ups. I don't know if I could have ran as fast through puddles either. At first I thought my stomach was upset because I was nervous, but it continued to feel upset throughout the day. I hope it doesn't feel like this tomorrow, and that it doesn't rain.

After I came back from formation I went back to bed. I wasn't able to sleep last night, so I was feeling sleepy right about that time. I slept until one in the afternoon. Know I wont be able to sleep at night, since I slept all day. As long as I get about five hours of sleep I will be fine.

Wednesday August 10, 2005

Once again I wasn't able to sleep. I think I finally fell asleep around three in the morning. It is very frustrating when you want to sleep but your body refuses. I laid in bed and dreamed with my eyes wide open. As a kid I always had great big and wild dreams, but it's not just a child thing. I still have wild dreams, I'm still a big dreamer. I would be very content if a fraction of my dreams came true.

It wasn't raining this morning. I was glad to get the PT test out of the way. I always get nervous, even though I was confident that I would pass. This time around I did more sit-ups and pushups than in any other PT test. My favorite event however is the two mile run. I prepared for the run the most. I was very disappointed when they gave me my time. I had ran thirty four seconds slower than my last recorded time. My time made me angry that I had put so much emphasis on my run, and to have ran slower. I finished third, so I didn't think I had done that bad. It could be that every one else is extremely slow.

I thought of several things that went wrong to justify my poor performance. To begin with I didn't quit smoking, but the guy who came in first is an avid smoker. I found my self running out of breath half way through the run. The weather was extremely humid, high humidity always slows you down. I haven't taken a shit in three days, and that was extra weight I was forced to run with. During the sit-ups I over exerted myself and my thighs took a beating. And finally, I only ran on the tread mill. I should have ran on the actual track. I had become accustomed to the tread mill, and it was a different feel on the concrete. I wasn't used to it.

There are many different factors that could have been the catalyst for my less than stellar performance. I do not know what my final score was, but I know its higher than my last PT test. I did improve, but I feel short from my goal. Six months from now I will get the chance to raise that score. I'll be better prepared next time.

My mom and my bothers went to New Mexico to spend the week with my dad. Now that he works in a different state they see less of him. My bothers have not started school, so until they do they can stay with my dad. Leaving his other job was a very brave move for my dad, especially leaving his family behind. He is not a risk taker, but he deserved a better job. It was time that he did something for himself. He always thinks of everyone else but himself. I am very proud of my father. I admire and look up to him. If I can become half the person, the man, the professional, half the brother, the son, half the friend, and father that he is it will be a great accomplishment for me. My father is an extraordinary person and an excellent role model.

Hopkins, Parsons and I had to go into work on our day off. It really sucked. The other two guys on shift have a different MOS, so there is certain equipment that is unique to our MOS. They are still not familiarized with our equipment.

Knowing that you would think that the section sergeant would schedule us on different shifts. Parsons and I always work the same schedule. If they would separate everyone who has the same MOS they wouldn't have to call people in. A lot of the stuff the sergeants do here doesn't make sense.

Thursday August 11, 2005

Sheena has made the transition from Las Vegas to Oregon. There was to much drama for her in Las Vegas, moving was a good way to start over. That's quite a change. That is definitely from one side of the spectrum to the other. I was able to talk to her today. We had not kept in touch for a while, since she was moving I figured she would be really busy.

I know Gabriel told me specifically not to tell Sheena that he was getting married, but I had to. I wanted to hear how she would react. She was surprised and shocked, and couldn't believe that I had waited this long to tell her. I was actually trying to be a good friend. I do not feel bad for telling her. Gabriel expects me to tell him everything that Sheena says, and Sheena expects the same. They have got to know that I do that. They can't be stupid enough to not know. At least I think they're not.

I talked to Gabriel after talking to Sheena, and he is unsure about getting married. I should have not even said anything to Sheena. Gabriel is very indecisive. The likelihood that he will go through with it is slim to none. He came to his senses. Getting married young is a huge mistake. He still doesn't know what he wants. In a couple of weeks he will be interested in some one else.

Victoria is upset because I only email her when she emails me first. If she goes a couple of days without sending an email I won't send her one until she emails me first. I told her she was as bad as me. When I was in basic training I wrote her very frequently. Out of all the letters I wrote she only responded twice. The only reason she emails me so often is because she gets bored at work. She also doesn't have to go out of her way to buy envelopes, stamps, and drive to the mail box to send off a letter. She told me that it would be nice to surprise her once in a while. I did feel compelled to call her and surprise her. Her phone was messed up. I wasn't able to talk to her.

I walked into a clean and good smelling room today. I was very surprised. My roommate decided to clean the room for once. It was about time. He didn't mop or clean the restroom, but at least he did something for once. I was getting tired of being the only one who cleaned the room.

Sunday August 14, 2005

I was extremely bored yesterday, there is nothing to do here. As much as I want to quit drinking I can't, because there is nothing else to do here. To solve my problem I went and bought two six packs of Bud Light. One for me and one for Parsons. We watched TV and had some cold ones, all that was left was a good barbeque. I wont be able to drink once UFL starts, so it was my last night of drinking for the month of August. I found out that the exercise wont start until Tuesday, so I will get the day off tomorrow. I do not plan on drinking today though.

One more Sunday that I haven't gone to church. I think this has been the longest time I've been without going to church. Going to church always made me feel better, and gave me extra strength to make it trough the week. I always was a positive person, now I'm the complete opposite. Primarily because I do not set time apart for God. Having a good relationship with God is an exceptionally imperative part of my life. Since I graduated basic training God has taken the back seat in my life. That's not how I want to live my life. I need spiritual guidance, it makes the journey through life so much easier. God knows my heart and my intentions. I know He is still with me and will not forsake me.

Eating out gets very expensive. I went and bought groceries, that will save me some money. I will also be eating healthier. Fast food is a good way to clog up your arteries and put on extra pounds. I will also get my mother of my back for spending to much money. I was already tired of eating the same food, there isn't a variety of places to order food from.

Monday August 15, 2005

I paid for a twenty dollar bus ride. At least that's what I think happened with the twenty dollars I lost. While I was paying for my food at McDonalds I noticed that I was missing twenty dollars. I had withdrawn forty dollars, and I had already used twenty for a calling card. When I opened my wallet all that was in there was a bunch of one dollar bills. I really do not know what happened to those twenty bucks. All I can think of was paying for the bus ride with that twenty dollar bill.

When we get on the bus there is a clear box that the passengers deposit their money in. I'm guessing that I pulled the twenty thinking it was a dollar, and placed it in the money container. I don't know if the bus driver noticed that I paid with a twenty dollar bill or not, but he only gave me change for a dollar. He received a really good tip this time. I will have to be more careful next time, and actually look at my bills before I give them away.

The Korean ladies give immaculate haircuts. They take their time and make sure that the customer is satisfied. They also give massages, but I don't like to get them. They are kind of aggressive. It's funny watching them give massages because it's so loud and extreme. I tried it once and the massage was more painful than enjoyable. They should definitely stick to cutting hair only.

In basic training we got haircuts every two weeks. The barbers almost scalped us every time they gave us a haircut, at least that's what it felt like. They dug the clippers into our skin. Our scalp was always red and irritated afterwards. The barbers would cut so many soldiers hair that they did not care if we were in pain or not, they simply cut as fast as they could. They always left uneven spots. The haircuts were only four dollars, so we got what we paid for.

In AIT the price of haircuts doubled, maybe because we were allowed to grow and keep more hair. The barbers could not shave everything off if we did not want them to. This time we could request a certain haircut, as long as it was within the military standards. They were not very skilled barbers. They always left one side higher than the other. Not once did I get a decent haircut from them. I think I did better when I cut my own hair. I would cut the sides and Gabriel would cut the back. I would cut Gabriel's hair, but if I messed up I could always expect for mine to be messed up as well. We figured that if we were going to pay for messed up haircuts might as well do it our self.

Tuesday August 16, 2005

UFL kicked of with an alert today. It was a very laid back alert, everyone was taking their time. I woke up around three-thirty this morning, because I did not want to be rushed. I could have gotten away with waking up at four-fifteen, and still been able to take my time getting ready. While I was sitting around waiting to sign in and to go to the company to pick up my weapon I called my grandma. Today is her birthday.

Work was busy, but not overwhelming. Everything was under control. I was able to use the phone and call Victoria. Looks like she is settling down with a guy who seems to be decent and deserving of her. I hope that things work out for her this time, even if that means that our deal would be called off. We have a better relationship as friends.

I talked to my sister. She is doing good, getting fatter. I am really excited about being an uncle. Maybe that will help me feel my age.

I also talked to my aunt Coco. Seems like the drama never ends in Big Lake. Relatives are fighting with each other, and my cousin is in jail. Craziness, I am glad that I am away from it all. Getting caught up in the drama is inevitable, even if you avoid it. The drama sucks you right in. Before you know it you are in the middle of everything and the talk of the town. Big Lake is cursed.

I was on the phone the whole morning, I hope it stays like that through out the exercise.

Wednesday August 17, 2005

The lieutenant, a civilian employee, and I got stranded at Camp Essayons. We went there to remove some equipment. When we arrived the lieutenant forgot to turn the lights off. We noticed that they were on about twenty minutes after we had arrived. We turned them off and did not think much of it.

When we were getting ready to leave the vehicle would not start. We tried pushing the vehicle, but that did not work. No one in the camp had jumper cables. We had to call for assistance. Two sergeants had to come and help us out. They took their time getting there too. It was extremely hot, and our BDUs are not exactly comfortable when it comes to hot, humid weather. When they got to our location they realized that they had forgotten the jumper cables. We drove all the way back to Camp Red Cloud to pick up jumper cables, then went back to Camp Essayons. We got the vehicle started, and what was going to be a hour task lasted all day.

I am very worried because I have not had a bowel movement in over a week. That is very odd for me, I'm used to having two bowel movements a day. After getting back from Camp Essayons I went to our post exchange to buy some laxatives. That should fix my problem. The suggested dosages is one to three pills. I took two. I figured that three pills were for the obese. It takes more pills to go through a bigger body. Laxatives should be part of an obese person's diet.

Thursday August 18, 2005

The laxative warnings suggested that a doctor be consulted if you do not have a bowel movement within twelve hours. Such occurrence could be the sign of a serious condition. I took the laxatives at approximately six in the evening. Six in the morning strolled along and still no bowel movement. I was concerned, but I did not want to ask my section sergeant if he recommended I see a doctor for my bowel troubles. I am a very honest and frank person, but such a question embarrassed me.

I then decided to call my sister, she had her share of bowel movements irregularities. She said that it was normal for her to have a prolonged absence of bowel movements. She had tried other forms of laxatives other than in tablet form and not given her any results. She told me not to be alarmed, but since I have medical coverage to see the doctor anyway.

My roommate suggested that I go as well, but said that the solution to my problem would probably result in an object being forced into my rectum. I choose to wait and see what was going to happen instead, and take more laxatives if necessary. Nothing was going to be inserted in my rectum.

Around noon I rushed to our unclean restroom at work. The unhygienic restroom did not seem to bother me. I actually did not have the choice to go to another restroom. I had a total of five bowel movements. I know it sounds absolutely gross and disgusting, but I had never been so ecstatic about taking a shit. I suppose not taking the optional three tablets could cause the process to take longer than twelve hours.

Good thing I chose not to say anything. It would have been a humiliating experience to see a doctor about something personal, that was only being delayed for unknown reasons. I spared my self the embarrassment and possible mockery.

Friday August 19, 2005

I talked to Gabriel, he told me about his friend's new potential hook up. The San Antonio native is a married latin woman. Her husband was stationed in Japan, but was deployed to Iraq. She stayed behind in Japan playing the single role. According to Gabriel her and her husband do not get along. She told Gabriel and his friend that she hates her husband. I suppose that hate is enough reason for her to cheat on him. What a slut! Her husband is not only away but risking his life in Iraq. The least she could do is divorce the guy. What really is sad, is if he dies she would get a quarter of a million dollars from his life insurance. It is very revolting to think that even though she has been unfaithful she could possibly walk of with a lump sum of money, in the event that he becomes a casualty. What a reward for opening her legs. I hope he comes home safe and dumps the whore.

I actually have no room to talk, because I was unfaithful to Ali. Not that it justifies being unfaithful, but we were not married. I guess you could say that I am as unrighteous as she is. Her scenario seems more morally wrong.

Saturday August 20, 2005

Today we participated in our NBC (Nuclear, Biological, and Chemical) Rodeo, which was a variety of training classes on the issue. I was an instructor with a

Katusa soldier. Our classes were on the application of the Mark 1 nerve agent antidote, how to protect yourself from nuclear, biological, and chemical injury/contamination when changing mission oriented protective gear, and the proper way to dawn our M40 series protective mask.

I instructed the class on how to protect yourself from nuclear, biological, and chemical injury/contamination when changing mission oriented protective gear. I was nervous the first time giving the class. I had a beneficial power point presentation in case I went blank, by the forth time I gave the class the use of the power point presentation was not needed. My class demonstrated how to decontaminate and exchange protective gear using the buddy system. Two of the soldiers who were in each class where used to demonstrate the roles of buddy number one and buddy number two. Buddy number one is responsible for the decontamination of his individual gear, his mask, and buddy number two's mask. He also helps him take off the contaminated trouser and jacket. He basically has to undo and untie every zipper and button, making sure he does not contaminate his buddy's undergarments. After that the roles are switched, and what buddy number one did for buddy two, buddy two will do for buddy number one.

We put a considerable amount of time in to the preparations of our classes. The preparation paid off, we were told that our class were the most interesting. No one was bored during our classes. I enjoyed giving the classes, it was something different for a change. Being in tech control can get old quick. Instructing was a useful way to break the routine. As much as it was fun, it was also tiring. I was not used to being on my feet all day.

All the instructors were given company coins from the commander, and congratulated on a well done job. The coins are a sign of appreciation, confirms and acknowledges our hard work.

The last time I gave the class was the worse. In the last group was all the section sergeants, platoon sergeants, and the first sergeant. I thought it was a good gesture that they took the time to go to our classes, even though they already were familiar with the information that was being put out. All they did was talk amongst themselves and paid no attention. I gave a class to an inattentive audience. I did not say anything because they were my superiors, but they are very anal when they are giving a class. They make sure that no one is talking and that everyone is being attentive. They sure do not lead by example. They contradict everything they preach to us. I though it was extremely rude, but I didn't care I wanted to finish and get it over with. I was ready to take a shower and take a nap.

Sunday August 21, 2005

For twenty dollars I buy a calling card, to use on my cell phone, to call home. That twenty dollar calling card will give me six hours of talk time. I have figured out that if I use my calling card on a DSN phone line I get doubled the talk time. Now I get to talk more frequently to my family, and other family members. Now I can communicate with my extended family not just my immediate family, like I was doing. Work is generally not that busy in the morning, so that's when I call home. I do not know if I am allowed to do so, but no one has said anything. I will continue to use the phone until I am told otherwise.

Today work was very slow, so they let a couple of us leave early. It was about time that they did something considerate. I had a hard time staying awake. What we do is hide behind the equipment and dose off. If the sergeants come in they won't see that we are asleep. Waking up at three-fifty in the morning is taking a toll on me, but there is only about twelve more days of the exercise left. The exercise will officially end on September second, so far it has not been as stressful as Warrior Storm. Thank God!

It bothers me when I lend someone something, and then they lend it to someone else. My roommate asked to borrow a movie. I bought, *Guess Who*, with Bernie Mac, Ashton Kutcher, and Zoe Saldana. He decided to let Hopkins borrow it, and Hopkins let our section sergeant borrow the movie. I hate when people do that. To begin with I don't like to lend movies or CDs, but since he is my roommate I made an exception. I am very meticulous about not getting the CDs scratched. Other people don't take good care of stuff that is not theirs. I will have to say no next time.

Tuesday August 23, 2005

Parson's has a back injury. They think it could be a slipped disc, and if that is the case he could get a medical discharge. He is going to have a series of appointments to determine the severity of his injury. The injury was caused when he fell of his skateboard during leave.

Today we had to get in MOPP level 4, for a total of four hours. MOPP level 4 consists of having our protective mask on, protective over garments, boots, rubber gloves, and our kevlar with protective cover. We were supposed to start at one, but we did not get into MOPP level 4 until about one-thirty. I did not wear the kevlar, because we were in doors. It sucked ass! The straps of the mask were digging into my head causing an intolerable headache. I think that who ever had my mask before was a heavy smoker, I could smell a strong cigarette odor. Wearing the mask made my skin burn. All the extra gear made it dreadfully hot and the sweat got into my eyes. The plastic cape of the mask created a puddle of sweat on my head and the sweat ran down my back. I had to pull the mask off, because it was so uncomfortable. The mask is so uncomfortable that I would actually consider not putting it on in the case of a chemical attack. I would much rather die then to endure the intense level of annoyance that mask brings. Needless to say I did not stay in MOPP level 4 the complete four hours.

After work my roommate and I went to the commissary to buy groceries. It was a exceptionally sunny afternoon, and when we walked out from the barracks we had to squint our eyes. It was bright outside, and as we tried to adjust our vision we walked past a lieutenant colonel. Obviously we did not see her rank and therefore did not salute her. Well the ass kisser who was with her scolded us for not doing so and she waited impatiently until we did so. Next time I will remember to look closely at everyone's collar to make sure I can see their rank, and salute if necessary. It is such a power trip for them. They get so offended if we do not salute them. Who cares! Get over yourself. Yes, we know that you are at the top of the food chain, but we do not care.

Friday August 26, 2005

I sent Ali an email to wish her a happy birthday. I have sent her two other emails that she has not responded to, chances are that she will not respond to this one either. I think that she might be really hurt because of what I did. I really regret the way I handled our relationship. In reality we did not have a relationship. We had been together a little over a month before I left for basic training. She lives in Midland so during that month and a half we did not see each other every day. It was more like every weekend. I do care about her, but I was not around her long enough to feel committed to her. For the most part of our relationship we were away from each other. It was more of a long distance relationship, which do not work. I did not want to be the one to break her heart. I was her first boyfriend and I ended up being a bad one. She even refuses to accept my friendship. It is better of this way, another year without seeing each other would have ended our relationship anyway. We had not been together long enough to endure the stress the distance can place on a relationship.

I have been thinking a lot about her lately. She is a wonderful person, she made me feel good about myself. She was never there so ultimately the relationship ended. I convinced myself to call her the other day, but there was no one home. I do not even know if she would have talked to me. I am curious to know where I stand in her life. I want to know if she still thinks about me, or if she has moved on and no longer thinks about me. I hope she emails me back.

Thursday August 27, 2005

Twenty three years old! I used to dream about being twenty one, and here I am today turning twenty three. I sure do not feel twenty three. I do not feel like an adult, there is still a lot of an adolescent in me. I sure do not look twenty three, everyone always thinks I am nineteen.

I must say that this has been the worse birthday ever. This is the first birthday I had to wake up early to go to work. I have been working since I was sixteen, and I have always managed to be off on my birthday. It's also the first birthday away from family and friends. Birthdays have always been memorable and significant. This was the first birthday I did not receive a gift, hug, or a party; not even a beer. Today has been like any other day.

When I lived in San Antonio my phone rang all day with family calling me to wish me a happy birthday. My mom called me last night, and my aunt wished me a happy birthday ahead of time. I called her a few days ago, but other than that no one called.

Since Victoria and I have been friends she has forgotten almost every birthday of mine. She would always remember days after. Today when I woke up I checked my email and there was a message from her. She wished me a happy birthday and told me how much she missed me. I was surprised! I was expecting her to forget once again. I was even thinking about what to tell her for forgetting my birthday. Victoria remembering my birthday has been the only highlight today.

Today we conducted CTT training, which was a joke. The classes were on how to care for an open wound, operate a radio, disassemble a M16, how to dismount an HMMWV when being ambushed, and a couple others. The classes we had were not prepared. It was obvious that there was no thought or preparation put into the classes. Some instructors did not even give the class. They signed off on our paper stating that they had, even though they did not. One instructor starts clearing on Monday, so training was not his priority. I did not care that they were inefficient in their training, this was a chance to get out of tech control.

After the training there was a reenlistment ceremony for one of our sergeants. During his speech he started crying. I had to try incredibly hard not to laugh. I wanted to point at him and laugh. Why would a grown man cry because he reenlisted? He did mention that he was not planning in doing so, but since he had a family to take care of it was the right thing to do. Maybe he was brought to tears because he is now stuck in the Army another four years. What ever the reason, he made a fool of himself for crying. The other sergeants were consoling him, but I know inside they were laughing. I was laughing.

There was a barbeque afterwards. The same as always hot dogs, burgers, chips, and sodas. The only difference was that there was no beer. Drink is what we usually do while we wait on the food. Today we simply waited by eating chips and puffing on cancer sticks. The barbeque ended at one in the afternoon, and we were released at that time. That was a nice treat. I'm tired of working everyday. Doing the training and getting off early made it seem like I had the day off.

Sunday August 28, 2005

We live in a country were we enjoy many freedoms. We have the right to worship what ever God we want, we can say what we want, we can do what ever the hell we want. Granted that it's legal. There is a reason why immigrants flock to this country. We are privileged to have been born in this country. There are millions of people who are less fortunate than us. There are children starving, countries being brought down by the AIDS epidemic, people who war is all that they know, and people who don't have homes. People who search the land fills for food, cloth, and hope that someone disposed of something that could be of great use to them.

As Americans we complain about the most insignificant issues. It is always we want this, we need this. We are a very selfish country. Greed is what drives us. We all have better solutions to what is going on in our country. We question the decisions that the president makes. Instead of praying for him we condemn him. The guy has a lot on his plate, but we are completely insensitive. We expect perfection from some one who will never achieve that. No one can deliver perfection.

We all want answers and solutions, but no one wants to do their part. The draft was the topic of a talk show today. They said that the country would not stand for a draft. That the president can not win the war on Iraq and that he does not even know how get out of Iraq. The Army is suffering, no one wants to sign up for the Army. Few people support what Bush is doing, I suppose that is why they choose not join. How are we going to win this war if there is a shortage of soldiers? We should earn what we have. Everyone should do a mandatory to years of service in the military. It is only fair, we should all do our part in insuring the safety of our country. We are all quick to judge, but to damn cowards to do our part.

Monday August 29, 2005

I have been avoiding having to drive in Korea. They say that it's the second most dangerous country to drive in. I was not successful in avoiding getting behind the wheel. Our lieutenant asked me to go to Yong Song with him, to pick up the lieutenant who is to replace him. I was very nervous. There was not to much traffic, which was especially helpful. Driving was not as dreadful as I expected it to be. I was driving a standard vehicle and not once did the vehicle stall on me. It was a smooth drive. After a while the nerves disappeared and cruised on through. I did not run any red lights, and I was looking forward to doing so.

The new lieutenant seemed like a genuinely nice guy. I got a good vibe from him. This will be his first official duty station. He was in the reserve and he now is active regular Army. He was friendly and talkative. He asked a lot of questions about work. He asked me if I liked it. My facial expression gave me away, so I could not lie. I told him I truly didn't. He seemed to be interested in why I did not like what I was doing, and offered suggestion to make it better.

When we arrived to Camp Red Cloud, I was invited to have lunch with them since I had done a great job driving. The lieutenant had called me inefficient the day before, I do not know if that was his unofficial way of apologizing for his comment. I did not care what the reason was, you can't beat a free meal. We met up with another lieutenant, he was not expecting me to come along. He seemed surprised to see me and asked if I was having lunch with them. He new lieutenant explained that I was. It was awkward I sat there and didn't say much. I did not want to intrude in their conversation. About fifteen minutes later the lieutenant that we met there asked me how I was doing. Kind of late considering I was sitting right in front of him. After a while the tension left and I found myself conversing with them. The lieutenant that asked me to go to Yong Song paid for my food. There is nothing better that a free meal. I was craving Mexican food, and I ordered chicken quesadillas. It was the closest thing to Mexican food that they had. They were satisfying.

After lunch I drove both of the lieutenants around all day. He did some in processing and settled in to his room. I did not even have to go to tech control, because by the time I was done driving them around it was time to get off shift.

Wednesday August 31, 2005

I am on force protection again. It was my roommates turn, but since he is on profile he can not do it. When we are on force protection we have to wear all of our gear, and his profile does not allow him to wear any of it. Honestly I think it is more of a theatrical performance rather than an actual injury. He has demonstrated to be a talented thespian. It pisses me off that he gets a way with so much, and the sergeants do not question his integrity. They believe all the lies he feeds them. The sergeants have no discernment to know when someone is lying to them.

Being on force protection during an exercise is some what convenient. That means I work four less hours a day. While the folks in tech control work twelve, I only work eight. So thanks Diaz for being a shammer. The weather is perfect now, it is not as hot as it was last time.

Today is family day for Steven. My aunt and uncle flew to South Carolina to see Steven. I can still remember family day, there was great anticipation to finally see my parents and siblings after two months of not seeing them. We woke up early that morning, finished packing the remainder of our stuff. Then we got into our freshly pressed BDUs and our nicely shined boots. The weather was cold that day so we had to wear our jackets. No one could really tell that we had ironed BDUs on.

We were marched to the building were our families were watching a video of what we did during basic training. The anticipation had reached its climax. The sergeants screamed at us for not being quite, but nothing could dampen my spirits. I was going to finally see my family.

They finally let our families out and there was a fast crowd of screaming parents. I was hoping that my mother wouldn't make a scene like the rest of the hysterical mothers. One of them was crying and screaming as she hugged her physically different son. This guy was over weight when he joined, and through basic training he shed the excess pounds. I hated that guy, but I was moved by his accomplishment. His mother was very proud, but she was making a scene.

I looked through the crowd of people, but could not see my family. I moved to higher ground to get a better view. I still could not spot them in the crowd. I figured that my father would be wearing a cowboy hat, so I looked for anyone who was wearing a cowboy hat. I spotted one, but he wasn't my father. Then I noticed that someone tugged on my jacket, it was my mom. She had sneaked up all the way to where I was, and I had not even seen her. I gave her a hug, I was extremely happy to see her. We walked over to where my father and my brothers and sister where. I was greeted with hugs from everyone. Seeing them warmed me from the cold weather. My dad made a joke saying that my mom was like a anxious goat searching for her lost little goat.

There was not much to do in Fort Jackson, and we were not allowed to go off post. We went to Burger King twice and cruised through the base. I did not matter that there was nothing to do. I was content with just being with them.

4

September

Thursday September 1, 2005

Force protection this time around is more monitored. We have sergeants checking up on us ensuring that we are doing our job and not asleep. The military police also make daily stops at the gate. They don't do much, other than stand there. We are supposed to check the trunks of all vehicles who exit the post, but rarely does anyone do it. Now they are checking to make sure that we are checking peoples trunks. We only check them while they are there, and as soon as they leave we stop checking the trunks. We have to make sure they are not stealing military equipment. We also make sure that they are not taking excessive amounts of beer, liquor, or cigarettes. The black market seems to still be a problem. Electronics, beer, liquor, and cigarettes are less expensive on post, and we do not pay tax. It has been known that soldiers purchase these items, and then sell them off post for a higher price than what they originally paid for. The price is still low enough to attract customers. The monetary profits of the black market can be very lucrative. The consequences are severe, but what are the chances that someone will get caught if we are not checking the trunks.

Today I received a birthday card in the mail from my parents. The card was a few days late, but it still served its purpose. Birthday cards always say exactly what you want to hear. Along with the card my mom sent pictures from there trip to New Mexico. To see recent pictures of my family was uplifting. I taped the pictures along with the others, that way I see them every day.

My brothers are packing on the pounds. Which is not good they are to young to be heavy. Kevin is only twelve and we already use the same pant size. Hopefully when he goes through his growth spurt he will loose the extra pounds. Tortillas will do that to you. Like I said they need to replace the tortillas with lettuce leaves.

Steven graduates today from basic training. We all counted the days from the first day we knew when graduation would be. It seems like that day will never come, and when it does you realize how fast it all went by.

Graduation was also one of the worse days of basic training. Graduation day was freezing cold. The cold caused my nose to run, and I could not wipe it. There I was with buggers running down my nose praying that they would not make it into my mouth. The drill sergeants made it very clear to us that if we moved we were going to stick out like soar thumbs. I did not want to be the one to stand out. Luckily graduation was over before the buggers reached my mouth.

Graduation was about an hour long, we were standing at the position of attention and parade rest, which is the modified position of attention. After five minutes at the position of attention your feet begin to feel very uncomfortable. The class A shoes are extremely uncomfortable to begin with. Not being able to move in class A shoes is twice as uncomfortable. I would casually lift my foot up, to relieve some of the pressure, and rotate the technique on each foot. Since I was one of the taller ones I was at the back of the formation. I knew that the audience would not see my very subtle movements. Our first sergeant was also standing at the back of the formation, and I could hear him telling us underneath his breath not to move. I knew he was not talking about me, because he would say it when I wasn't moving. I did not even hear the graduation ceremony. All I heard was "stop moving," along with some curse words in there. Curse words were the primary words in his vocabulary.

What made every one mad on graduation day was that we could not leave until one in the afternoon. Graduation was over by eleven, and the other two hours we waited impatiently. Staying there doing nothing was retarded. That was the time that everyone got the chance to take pictures and exchange phone numbers. Once one rolled around our parents were able to sign us out. Everyone else who did not have a parent to sign them out did not leave until Monday, and graduation was on a Thursday. I bet it sucked to be them.

AIT graduation was very different compared to basic training. Since there were only about twenty of us, the graduation was held in doors in a conference room. We had chairs to sit on. We did stand briefly, but for the most part we sat. It was on a hot day, but the air conditioner certainly helped out. The graduation ceremony was about forty-five minutes long. They stretched the time by having a guest speaker. We also stood at the front of the room one at a time and said our name, MOS, and where we were going to be stationed at. After that we shook a couple of hands and received a fake rolled up diploma. Actually it was just a blank rolled up paper, tied with an orange ribbon.

We were released immediately afterwards. We took off to a go cart place. We bought some liquor and some fountain drinks at a convenience store. We poured some of the drink out and filled it back up with some liquor. Oldest trick in the book, but it works every time. After that we went to the opening night of *Star Wars*. I had not seen any of the other movies, but I went anyway since it was our last time hanging out together. The movie was boring and Melissa, Stewart Southern, and I fell asleep. Gabriel is a huge *Star Wars* fan and he was convinced that I would become one as well after seeing the movie. Sheena and him were in a different theater, so they did not know we were asleep. We got him all pumped up by telling him *Star Wars* was the greatest movie we had ever seen. Then he bragged about how he was right about me becoming a *Star Wars* fan. I could not having him bragging to much so we finally told him that we slept. He was pissed off, when we told him we slept. It was hilarious.

Friday September 2, 2005

Actually it sounds more like "suck on a nun." I hate sounding off to "second to none." Half of the people don't even hear us because their windows are rolled all the way up, and are blasting their music. Other than the die hard soldiers, no one cares to hear our motto. When I see that their windows are not rolled down, I only salute. They are not going to hear our motto anyway. I am sure not going to yell it at the top of my lungs either.

UFL is officially over, thank God. UFL was actually not that terrible. I was expecting worse. Now we can go back to working four days out of the week. We can watch movies at work and not having to worry about the exercise. We can also go back to drinking. The drinking will have to wait until tomorrow after noon. No one is allowed to drink until then. I do not know who had that bright idea, but it does not affect me. Even if I wanted to drink I can't since I am on force protection. I could probably drink one or two and get away with it. There is no such thing a just one beer for me, I won't stop until I am drunk.

Saturday September 3, 2005

I have found that reading a book during force protection makes the time go by considerably faster. I am reading *The Secret On Ararat*, an incredible page turner. The book is written by Tim LaHaye and Bob Phillips. Tim LaHaye is the author of the *Left Behind* series. The book I am reading is the second installment of his new *Babylon Rising* series. This book is excellent, I will definitely have to read the first one and the third one that will be out this fall. I will have to look for the first book at Camp Casey because they do not have it here. I think they have more of a variety of books over there.

I received an email from Victoria that said, "Hi Ramon its me again, I just realized that every guy I've ever been with never really loved me at all. Isn't that awful? It was all just a lust issue. All physical attraction. That's what it was with Renee…I think that you are the only guy that has sincerely loved me for me, and I have never even slept with you! I don't think anyone will ever love me like that! I'm so stupid. Isn't that weird."

The email made me laugh, but it was not a ridiculing laugh. It was an unexplainable laugh. It's funny, because a few days ago I had told myself that I was already over Victoria. Then I receive this email that confirms that my feelings for her are otherwise contradictory to what I believed. I think that her relationship with Renee is not going as she would have planned. I do not how to interpret this email, but it stirs a whirlwind of emotions with in me. It really does not matter what any of us feel for each other. We are merely great friends, and relationship between the two will always stay that way. I am here and she is on the other side of the world. What we feel does not matter. I don't think she is saying that she wants to be with me either. I am probably reading to much into the message.

Sunday September 4, 2005

Last night during force protection one of us accidentally set off the panic alarm. I did not even know that we had a panic alarm. Someone must of brushed up against and set it off. We did not know we had done so until the military police arrived. They asked us what was going on. "With what," I said. Then he explained that the alarm was set off. They tried calling us to make sure that everything was okay, but the Korean security guard was on the phone with his wife. They were not able to get through, they should really consider getting call waiting. All the military police did was reset the alarm. I had to write a statement on what had happened. I felt like I had witness a crime or something.

There was a parade of drunken soldiers last night as well. I had never noticed how appalling they smell, and they got so close to talk to us. They breath heavier when they are drunk. I wanted to say "back off buddy," because I could not hold my breath that long. I found my self holding my breath countless times. All they want to do is talk instead of getting to where ever it was that they were going. One of them gave everyone a hug. Drunks have a tendency to get very touchy feeling. Another soldier did not see the metal rope, that keeps anyone from driving through past curfew hours, and fell on the ground. His buddies had to help him up, he couldn't even walk straight. I wanted so hard to laugh, but I kept my military bearing. They definitely make the shift very interesting and amusing. Drunks provide great entertainment.

Monday September 5, 2005

I have noticed that the weather has begun to change. The nights are a bit chili, we had to turn on the heater at the force protection hut. I am really not looking forward to the winter. I would much rather be dripping in sweat than be cold. I hope that I won't be stuck on force protection in mid winter, that would be awful.

We were serenaded by the contestants of Military Idol. We could hear their poor singing efforts from the back gate. I think it is ridiculous that the Army is doing their version of American Idol. Out of all the contestants that I heard sing, no one sounded great. Yeah some could carry a tune, but in order to make it you have to be great. I do not know what the winner gets, the finals will be conducted in Fort Gordon. I seriously doubt that the winner will get a recording contract. If that is the case they would have to get out of the Army. You can not have a successful signing career and be in the Army at the same time. I am sure that if the winning person received a recording contract that the media would have been doing some sort of coverage. I have not seen anything on television about this event. The auditions are taking place all over every post. If they are doing them way out here I wonder if they will also be doing them in Iraq.

Before my second shift of force protection I bought a six pack of Coronas. I have not drank in three weeks. I could not resist waiting any longer to drink a beer. A six pack won't get me drunk. My alcohol tolerance level probably dropped, but not enough to make a six pack get me drunk. They were incredibly refreshing.

Tuesday September 6, 2005

I had no idea that the damage caused by hurricane Katrina was so devastating. Until today I had not seen the coverage of the hurricane damage. The devastation was overwhelming, watching dead bodies float in the water and laying in the empty streets. Laying there is very humiliating, their bodies are left unattended as if they were road kill. The stories the survivors tell are truly horrific. One would never think that such a catastrophic event could happen in our nation. The situation is especially heartrending.

Seems like Bush is always getting negative press. The broadcast I was watching was criticizing the way president Bush handled the situation. They also talked about Kanye West comments on the issue. He said something along the lines that

Bush did not care about black people. He was also disappointed with the media's coverage. The blacks were accused of looting, but the whites were only looking for food, not looting. Basically all the shows I saw asked the same question, had the population been predominately white, middle class people they would have received help faster. I have not been following the coverage enough to have an opinion. I do think that the fact that *Time* magazine named Kanye one of the most influential people in the world, went to his head. I think Kanye is always over confident and extreme in what he says. He needs to put his feet back on earth. In the September issue of *Blender* magazine he was quoted on the following: "the last album was ground breaking now the process is to strive for greatness. Anybody who ain't respecting me as an artist now might as well bash their heads into the wall for being stupid. It's hard trying to find something that I'm not good at." his ego has gotten to big for him to carry, I think his comment was completely bias. He seems to very close minded, and if someone does not think like him they are wrong. That is the impression that he gives. It is kind of extreme to blame this on racism.

Wednesday September 7, 2005

This time around during force protection everyone was ten to fifteen minutes early, like they should be. They had to spoil it on the last night. Our relief was fifteen minutes late. It wasn't that bad, but on that last day of force protection you just want to be done with it. Five minutes can feel like an eternity when you have to wait past the end of your schedule. Especially knowing that I am going to be off for the next four days. I deserve to be off. I hope that I do not have to do force protection during the winter. I do not like being cold. I would much rather be drenched in sweat than be cold.

I received another birthday card, this time it was from my sister. She sent the card the same day my mother sent hers. What's funny is that she sent the card on express mail, and it took longer to get here. It still served its purpose. I think that was the first birthday card I've received from my sister. It meant more to me than she would know.

Today I had the chance to talk to Justin and Cynthia. I had made several attempts to communicate with them, but I would get their voice mail every time. I called Cynthia and she placed Justin on three way. She said that he would not answer the phone if he did not recognize the phone number. My only chance to talking to him was if she called him instead.

I have known Justin and Cynthia since we were kids. We graduated the same year. During school Justin and I were not friends. It wasn't until our senior year that we actually became friends, for the most part he was merely an acquaintance. Cynthia, James, and I had planned that we would live together in San Antonio. We were all applying to the same school. We took our ACT on the same day, and the results for Cynthia and James where a bit embarrassing. I think that was what discouraged James from going to college. Cynthia retook the parts that she did not pass and was still determined to go to school.

Like I have said before nothing works out the way you plan it, especially during high school. Cynthia enrolled in Angelo State University in San Angelo, Texas. James moved to Midland, and started working with his brother. I moved to Midland as well, and after two months moved to San Antonio. The only one who stuck to his plan was Justin. He went to school in New Mexico on a tennis scholarship. He did not like it there to much and after his freshman year was over he moved to San Antonio with his sister.

When Justin moved to San Antonio we started hanging out. We became good friends. Around the time he was looking to move out, was the time that I had to let the leasing office if I was going to sign for another six months or move out. I suggested to Justin that we should get an apartment together. It would be cheaper for the both of us. He agreed and we moved to the north side of San Antonio.

He was a good roommate. Our rooms were on opposite ends, so rarely did we have to put up with each others noise. We never had to fight about anything. I think we were both skeptical about signing a one year lease, because we didn't know if we were going to get along or not. It worked out, we had a lot of the same friends. We did not have to worry about having someone over that the other did not like.

Talking with them and catching up was enjoyable. They are two, of the few, friends I have left from high school. Now that I am in the Army I don't see my friends very much. I talk to them once in a while, but true friends will always be there. Once I got out of high school I was able to see who my real friends were, and I made some new ones along the way. It is important to have people in your life that you can really trust.

Thursday September 8, 2005

Since I was off today I decided to go to Camp Casey. They have more places to buy stuff. I called a cab to take me to the bus station. When he picked me up he asked me where I was going. I told him where, and he offered to take me himself. It's only two dollars to take the bus, of course I said no. I told him to stop by the ATM before taking me to the bus station. Once I got back into the cab he told me that he had seen the bus leave already, and I would have to wait another hour before the next bus would leave. I did not know whether or not to believe him, but I did not want to wait another hour to take the next bus.

Hesitantly I told him he could take me to Casey. I got the feeling that he was lying, so he could make twenty-two bucks. Had he just taken me to the bus station he would have only made a dollar and eighty cents. I would have given him a twenty cent tip, and it would have been two dollars. Twenty-two dollars sounds better than two, I would have lied as well.

During the ride he told me that he was saving money to move his family to Ohio. He has a brother there, and in three years he will leave to the states. He said that he was thankful for having us. By driving the soldiers to their destinations he is able to save the money he needs to move to the United States. He is currently taking English classes, he wants to be able to speak more fluently. His English was somewhat choppy. I managed to understand what he was saying. I am getting better at deciphering what Koreans are saying when they speak.

He offered me a cigarette, of course I was not going to refuse. It was as if he had read my mind, or maybe he saw me eying his cigarettes. Korean cigarettes are very different from American cigarettes. You have to take a longer drag to actually get a good hit from a Korean cigarette. I think they have less nicotine.

Friday September 9, 2005

I received an e-card from Ali. I had not opened the email, because at first glance the email address was unfamiliar to me. I was very surprised when I opened the email and saw that it was from her. I was not expecting her to send me an email. The email said, "Hello Ramon! I hope you had a wonderful birthday! I hope it was full of fun, surprises, happiness, and faith. Take joy in all the small and big moments of your life. Don't let time pass you by and eat you away. I wish you the best. Thank you for your wishful thinking. Sorry I sent it late. May God keep blessing you and may He guide you, protect you, and keep you company. Take care and God bless. Sincerely, Alicia Lopez."

I am glad that she finally responded to my emails, I was beginning to think that she hated me. The email wasn't an actually response, because she did not address anything that I have talked about in the previous emails. The email was only wishing me a happy birthday. Her reasons for not talking to me are justifiable, but this email tells me that she still cares. She has to care otherwise she wouldn't have sent that e-card.

My sister is having a boy. My mom was somewhat disappointed, she had been hoping for a baby girl. There hasn't been a little girl that close since my sister. My sister was not hoping for a specific gender. Since this is her first, the gender does not matter to her. She is excited either way.

I am really pumped! I will be an uncle, a very adult term. Maybe I will start acting like an adult. Maybe a nephew will help me feel my age. My dad says he is still to young to be a grandfather. He said that when the baby was old enough he was going to tell him that they are cousins. I am really looking forward to playing the role of an uncle. That role is to spoil the hell out of him. What ever mommy and daddy wont get, I will get. When ever they say no, I will say yes. It's upsetting that I will not be able to see him until six months later.

Saturday September 10, 2005

Last night was another Apache night. Hopkins, Quinn, and I went after drinking a few in the barracks. Getting a buzz before going to the bar is a must, because drinks are ridiculously expensive. I didn't stop at the buzz, I think I was already drunk by the time we left the barracks. Saying exactly what's on my mind, without holding back, is a sign that I am drunk.

Apache was kind of dull this time around. Kelly quit, consequently she wasn't there. There was a new girl working, but they have not given her an American name yet. She told me her name, but it was to complex to even try and remember it. After two drinks we left the bar.

We ended up at a bar I had never heard anyone talk about before. There wasn't very many people there either, but it was early. A sergeant from our company meet us there. He's cool, but he looked like he had just walked off the set of a rap video. This sergeant is white, so you can imagine what he looked like. After another two drinks we left the bar, by this time I was trashed. I was pissed off because I was bored. Quinn and this sergeant always brag about how they always have a great time and meet so many girls. I thanked them for being lame this time around. I went off on how un-cool they were. I was drunk so I did not think twice about what I was saying, but I am sure I would have said that if I was sober anyway. I think the sergeant got offended, because when we got to the club Hopkins told me to stop running my mouth. The sergeant told Hopkins that I need to watch my mouth. He is lucky I didn't make fun of him for what he was wearing. That was the real joke, and that wouldn't have been me being sarcastic. That was then plain truth.

This morning everyone asked me why I was picking fights with sergeants, Hopkins ran his mouth. He even video taped the incident. I didn't even noticed that he was video taping us. I have no desire to see it.

September 11, 2005

Yesterday we had a mandatory barbeque. I detest everything that is mandatory, especially if it's something recreational. I do not think that we should be forced to participate in social gatherings. I am assuming that the motive for the barbeques being mandatory is creating a bonding environment for everyone. The more united a company is, the better we're off. There is always conflict and there will always be conflict. I am more than willing to get along with everyone. I may not like you, but I will get along with you.

Parsons and Hopkins came this morning and very abruptly woke me up. They said that I had to attend the barbeque and that we were late already. They didn't even give me the time to take a shower. I put some clothes on, washed my face, brushed my teeth, and I was out the door. We weren't late, there were only three other people there. The food wasn't even on the grill yet.

I needed to do something, I wasn't going to sit and wait for the food with nothing to do. It was probably not the best choice, but I went and bought some beer. I woke up with an extreme hang over, I was probably still drunk from the night before. I had finished three beers before the food was ready. At this point any senses of soberness I had was completely drowned with the three beers I drank. Everyone was already there by this time. By choice or by force, but they were there.

I could have left after I ate, but I figured if I was forced to be there to begin with might as well stick around. I continued to drink, and the more I drank the more I talked. I like to say what's on my mind. I probably said to much, but I couldn't leave the barbeque. My roommate left with a new female soldier, that arrived a couple of days ago, to Seoul. He locked the door to the room with my keys inside. I was also having a good time. The sergeants asked me a ton of questions about everything and everyone, hoping that in the drunk state that I was in I would say something to incriminate someone. I was drunk, not stupid. I can still read people when I'm drunk. I played into their little game. I was having a good time, and so was everyone else. I was making everyone laugh. They were surprised to see that I had so much to say. I'm usually quite and stick to myself. I wanted to stay under the radar. So much for that.

The barbeque started at eleven in the morning, and I stayed out there until eight in the evening. One of the sergeants had to get the spare key to my room to let me in. I passed out, I didn't feel my roommate come in. I was gone.

Today everyone looks at me and laughs. I talked a whole lot of nonsense, I must admit. People who normally did not talk to me, are know talking to me.

Why do people always avoid people who are quite and reserved? No one cares to know anyone like that. Up until now I was quite, that's what I wanted people to think. There is a few who knew the loud me, but for the most part everyone thought I was shy. Now that I made a fool out my self and made people laugh, people start talking to me.

I wonder how many great people we missed out on getting to know, simply because they were different from what we were used to. It is not fair to push people way because they are different. We all have a different story to tell, we all can learn from each other.

I am disgusted with they way society works. People are fake and seek only what will profit them. I try to stop and say to myself, "how can I help this person out." "How can I make a difference in this person's life." I have made mistakes in they way I dealt with certain people, and I wont let that happen again. I like to study people and do certain things to see how they will react, and so far I am not impressed.

Monday September 12, 2005

I thought it was strange that I have been here three months and have not been tested for drug use. When I arrived in Georgia for AIT we were tested two days after being there. I must have been tested a total of four or five times within a fourth month period. Every time I was tested it was as uncomfortable as the previous time. The uncomfortable feeling never left. We never had warnings. We were taken into the day room, and we would start drinking water. The sooner we had to go, the sooner we would get out of there.

Whoever had to go use the restroom would get in line first. Two were taken in at a time, with two drill sergeants. We had to hold our bottle above our shoulder and make it visible at all times. We had to drop our trousers and underwear below our knees, then tuck our shirt under our chin. We could not stand to close to the urinal, the drill sergeants had to be able to see us piss in the bottle.

Regardless of how bad you have to piss, when you have someone staring at your penis it makes it extremely difficult to piss. It would take a while of forcing and trying to concentrate on making the urine begin to flow. There is actually no technique in those situations. I tried concentrating, not concentrating, but every time it took a while to get the piss flowing. Once the urine was flowing you only hoped that it was enough to fill the bottle.

Sometimes there would be guys who stayed there for hours. The females usually didn't have a hard time pissing on view and demand. Whoever wasn't able to piss, the drill sergeants made them run around the building a couple of times. I don't know if that works, but it gets your mind off the pressure of having to piss.

Today I was told around five-twenty in the morning that I had to attend PT formation, because I would be having a urine analysis. Right before the sergeant knocked on my door to tell me about the urine analysis, I was going to go to the restroom to take a piss. I was going to hold it, but I had to go very urgently. PT formation wasn't until five-forty five, I didn't think that I could hold it that long. I figured that by the time I had to actually piss in the bottle I would have to go anyway.

After formation we went to the company, on the way over to the company I drank a whole canteen of water. By drinking that much water I would definitely have to piss.

In the Army waiting is usually a requirement. By the time everything was set up, I was about to piss on my self. When it was finally my turn, I went in by myself to the restroom. With a sergeant of course. The sergeant stood a few steps behind me, so he wasn't actually watching. I pulled out my penis and placed the bottle below it. I managed to get a little trickle of piss out immediately, but then I froze. I had to piss really bad, but I could not piss in the damn bottle.

I told the sergeant that maybe letting the water run in the sink would help. He turned on the water, and some piss trickled down. After that I froze again, and it wasn't enough piss either. I couldn't force my self, because I had to take a shit. I was afraid that if I tried to force myself to piss that I would shit on myself.

Finally one last squirt of piss came out, and it was enough to fill the bottle. Soon after the bottle was sealed and I signed the usually papers, I ran towards the barracks. I rushed to my room and went straight to the restroom. I really had to go, but when someone is watching it's always difficult.

Today I was confronted about my drunken confessions about a specific soldier. I supposedly said something incriminating about this soldier. She confronted me about what I said in a very passive aggressive way. I have no recollection of saying anything about her that night, her name was never even brought up. The person who told her this, in my opinion has no credibility. I think she just pinned this on me thinking since I was drunk enough I would not remember what I said. I remember exactly what I said, and I can bet on my innocence. I feel terrible because, I don't think she believes me, but oh well. That's what I get for putting myself in that predicament.

Tuesday September 13, 2005

It has been raining all day today. It's nothing like the rain in Texas. The times it rains it is usually accompanied by a thunder storm or dust storm. When it rains here it's a continuous steady rain. The rain falls very calming, soothing I should say. Since it rains so often the soothing effect transforms into annoyance.

Today we attended a reenlistment meeting with our first sergeant. He wanted to talk to us about the options we have when it comes to reenlisting. Since this is my first term in the Army, and if decide to reenlist I have more options than those who already reenlisted once before. We have the choice of our duty station and a possible bonus. We can also attend college for six months and get paid for it. That would be all I would be doing, simply attending school.

There are many options that make reenlisting very alluring, but it is entirely to soon for me to decide. There are days when I say I'm getting out, there days when I feel like I would like to stay in longer. Right now I am undecided. I don't know how I'll feel once it is time for me to decide.

One thing is for sure. I will not get out of the Army, and end up the way I was before I joined. If my economic situation does not get better, then I will not get out. I will not get out of the Army to struggle. I've had enough of the struggling. The Army provides financial stability, and for me that is enough to want to stay in. I do not want to live pay check to pay check or depend on my parents.

Right now, I have no clue. Reenlisting is something I have to pray about. That is something that I have to think about. I have a couple of years to sleep on it. I also want to see what my next duty station will be like. I can not make a decision without experimenting what it would be like to be some where else. It could be better than what it is here, and it could be worse. I am glad to know that I actually have options, and I can reenlist on my terms.

Wednesday September 14, 2005

On of the emails that Victoria sent me today stated that she was upset. On one of the emails I sent her, I did not end it with the usual I love you. I did that on purpose to see if she would notice or even cared. To my surprise she did notice, and she does care. I sent her an email apologizing. She said she would forgive me this time.

I get so many mixed signals from that girl. Sometimes I get the impression that a part of her wants me. There are times when she makes it very clear that we are only friends. I know she cares for me and loves me, but I would like to know what holds her back. It could be that I am half a world away. I go through this in my head over and over, each time coming up with a different conclusion. I am never satisfied with any conclusion that I come up with.

I called her once she got off work, the sergeant on shift had conveniently left. I didn't have to worry about being on a personal phone call or having my conversation listened to. She was very happy to have heard from me, as I was to hear from her. Hearing her voice brings a warm feeling inside. I was used to speaking to her on a day to day basis. The few times I do talk to her now, I cherish dearly.

She was making lasagna with her sister Rebecca. I pitied myself for not being there, they make very delicious lasagna. Anything homemade at this point sounds good, even beans. There is nothing better than a home cooked meal.

Her relationship with Renee is officially over. I was relieved. I knew it would end the way it did, but I wanted her to find that out on her own. Sometimes we have to go through devastating situations to learn a thing or two. She will be fine.

We talked about our friendship. It has survived distance, struggles, and sabotage. I admitted to have personally sabotaged our friendship. Sometimes I felt like not having her in my life would be easier to deal with. Out of sight out of mind type of thing. That never worked, I always felt guilty. She needs me as much as I need her. We agree that we are in each others life for a reason. We have yet to know what will become of us. I was glad I got to talk to her, her voice was comforting.

I also talked to my mother. She told me she talked to Ali. I was curious as to why she would call my mother. My mom said she called her to invite her to her wedding. I immediately ask, "who."

My mom said that she was getting married to a doctor that she was working with. I was overwhelmed with an inconsistent feeling. I did not know exactly how to feel. My mom asked me if I cared that she was getting married. I didn't know what to answer. All I said was that it could not be true. If she was getting married, she would have not emailed me for my birthday. She would have certainly told me about it. I think that she would have told me to stop emailing her because she was getting married.

Just as I suspected, she was lying. My mom wanted to see how I would react. I know my mother to well, she always tries to pull shit like that. I also know that Ali would not rush into something as important as marriage. She takes that very seriously. Marriage is a big commitment.

I do find it odd that she called my mother. Why? Why would she care to keep in touch with my family? She broke up with me. She doesn't respond to my emails, but somehow she finds the time to call my mother. My mom said that she wanted to know how she was doing, and how my sister's pregnancy was going. If she wanted to know that she could have called my cousin. Gabrielle and Ali have been friends since Ali was fourteen. Gabby would have told her that.

Ali used to baby sit my aunts kids when we went out to the clubs. That is how I met Ali, she was my aunts babysitter. When I first met her I thought she was cute, but she was fourteen. I didn't think anything about being with her, she was a kid. She was very shy and she seldom talked to me. I would have to force a conversation out of her. Once I moved from Midland to San Antonio I lost all contact with her. She was the babysitter, I really did not care to keep in touch with her. She was a kid.

Three and a half years later I ran into her in the mall in Midland. I was not sure if that was her, so I did not talk to her. She was know a young woman. She was very different from the girl I knew. She did not recognize me either. She called Gabby that day and told her she tough she had seen me. Gabby gave her my phone number, and she called me. We started talking, one thing led to another, and we started dating. Who would have known that I would end up dating my aunt's babysitter.

Why call my mom? I though that maybe she wanted to know about me without having to get in touch with me. Maybe I am reading to much into this. My mom said that she did not ask for me. She said that they are friends, that justifies the call. My mom grew very fond of her. That is reason enough for my mother to want to stay in touch with her. My mom has her number now, and plans to keep in touch with her.

I called Victoria and asked her what she thought about the whole ordeal. She said that she would keep in touch with her ex boyfriend's parents. That just because our relationship is over does not mean that their relationship has to be over. But why! There is to much of an age difference for Ali and my mother to be friends. Girls are so difficult to understand.

Thursday September 15, 2005

The Korean civilians who work with us always smell like garlic. I have no idea why there breath always smells like that. Maybe the Korean food makes your breath smell like garlic all the time. I don't think that brushing their teeth works, because when they come in the morning they already smell like garlic. Some days the smell is worse than others, but every time I am around them I smell garlic. Sometimes the smell is so repulsive that I have to hold my breath or step back. The smell is exceedingly unpleasant. I don't know if they are aware that they smell like that. The smell is horrific, they should do some sort of detoxification.

The fumes that are released from their mouths are very toxic. The smell is unbearable.

I talked to my mom today, and she confessed that Ali did ask for me. Why would she ask my mom about me when she can ask me herself? It does not make sense to me. Sometimes I want to call her, but I do not think that she wants to talk to me. If she wanted to talk to me she would at least send me an email. I don't know what to think. Girls are extremely confusing, and that is an understatement.

I had to attend a mandatory hail and farewell. What they do is welcome the people who within that month joined our company, and say farewell to those who will be leaving. The hail and farewell took place at Mitchell's. Mitchell's is a restaurant, bar, and club all in one. Mitchell's is the only establishment of this type on post. Since it was mandatory all of the Katusas where there. Everyone ordered food and drinks, and since the Katusas barely makes any money they just sat there. I do not like for people to watch me eat. Unfortunately I couldn't buy them all food, but I did buy three of the Katusas food. I feel awful that they do not have the money for simple things like food.

I was under the impression that the sergeant we had met at the bar that one night was mad at me. I tried to avoid him, but he talked to me. He asked me if I remembered that night. How could I forget, everyone talked about that night thanks to Hopkins. I apologized, and he told me not to worry about it. I think that Hopkins made a bigger deal out of the issue than it actually was.

Friday September 16, 2005

I received two emails from Victoria today. In both of the emails she left out the I love you. I do not know if she did that on purpose, or if she simply forgot. The emails had no substance to them. It seemed that she wrote them in a hurry. In one of them she accused me of regretting breaking up with Ali. I did not brake up with Ali, she was the one who dumped me. She said that I still wanted her back, and that Ali wants me back as well. Somehow she knows more than me.

I responded with the following email, "Even if I did want her back, I could never be. I am here and she is in the states. So there is no point to even worry or care about what she wants. It's a waste of time to even try to work something out. I do not care. She can be best friends with my mother for all I care. It is not going to change the fact that I am a half a world away. Besides, I had to lie about talking to you. She did not want for me to talk to you. I am not going to be with some one if they do not want you in my life. You are priority. You have always been there, and you will continue to always be there. So until I can find someone who is okay with that, I'll just stick to myself."

I am very puzzled. I do not know what to think. My friendship with Victoria is very important, but will I ever find someone who will be okay with that. Knowing that my feelings for her have been more than that of a friend. I make her my priority, but she has never done that for me. Why should I sacrifice finding true happiness by waiting for her? She has not asked me to wait for her. I am doing this on my own account, and for what.

Ali is a great girl, and sometimes I do think that I messed it up. There is no reason for me to dwell on that situation. Whatever the case may be, I am here not there. Being away always complicates things. How was I supposed to have known what to do, or what to do now? It is all to complicated.

Sunday September 18, 2005

My CQ shift began at nine this morning, and it will continue until tomorrow, ending at nine in the morning. CQ stands for charge of quarters. What we do is make sure that the building is secure. Who ever goes off post has to sign out with the person on CQ, and if someone brings a visitor into the building they have to sign in as well. CQ is basically twenty four hours of watching movies, reading books, or any form of entertainment that will keep you awake for twenty four hours.

I struggled staying awake the first four hours of my shift. I recently bought a portable DVD player. I wanted to watch the second season of *One Tree Hill*, but it would not play it. Since I could not figure out why the DVD player would not play the discs I watched *Stripperella*. Before that I tried numerous times to try and make the DVD play the discs. Once I was done watching *Stripperella*, I tried to play the discs again. I tried several times and it would not play the discs. I was furious I was determined to exchange the DVD player. I could not figure out why it would play everything else and not *One Tree Hill*. I knew that the discs were not defective because the play station would play them. Finally I tried one last time and it played the disc.

It turns out that you have to push the play button. I felt so dumb. For hours I tried to figure out what the problem was. It never occurred to me that I had to push the play button. I never had to press that button for any other DVD, it would automatically play. From now on I will remember to always press the play button. That would have saved me so much frustration. I was tempted to throw the DVD player against the wall. I cursed at it and called it cheap, and I was the one at fault. I'm glad that I figured that out before returning the DVD player. It would have been very embarrassing for them to tell me that all I had to do was push the play button.

Wednesday September 21, 2005

I hate the person that I am when I am drunk! There are sides to everyone that only surface when alcohol becomes the fulcrum. I wonder if that is who we really are. Alcohol brings out the worse in people. The negative aspects of our lives are suppressed by soberness. We do not know who people really are until we see them drunk. That is not fair to say, because some people do not drink. Each time that we drink we react different. If that is true, that means that the people who do not drink we will never truly know.

When people are drunk we can sometimes see what they hide and harbor inside. We all have our demons and face our own battles. If we left alcohol out of the equation, our solution would be easier to find. Alcohol never solves anything. Alcohol always makes things more convoluted. We all search for answers, and they are closer to us than we know. We look in all the wrong places. I do not like the person I am when subdued by alcohol. The obvious solution would be not to drink. It is tremendously difficult, even though the solution is that simple.

The only reason for not deciding and going through quitting drinking is that something within me craves the dark side. The book of Romans says that if I do what I hate to do. It is no longer I who does it, but sin living inside me that does it. Does that not make me accountable for what I do? I am accountable for the sin in my life. So it is my fault for living a sinful life. The answer is so clear. Get rid of the sin, and the problem vanishes. It is easier said than done.

We have the answers to our problems, but we choose to ignore them. We try to find loopholes and justification for what we do. We are attracted and turned on by wickedness. It brings an adrenaline rush. What is forbidden is always more desirable. Once we face the consequences of our actions, clarity and reality sinks in. That is when we realize how wrong we were, even though we knew all along. We have the power to choose our destiny, yet we always complain about where we are in life. It is completely and solely up to us to change what we do not like. We do nothing about it. Where ever I find myself ten years from now, I will have myself to thank. It is all up to me.

Thursday September 22, 2005

By working in tech control we miss out on sergeant time training. The only time I was required to go was when I was in processing. The other time I took part in sergeant time training was when it was MOS training, but we have not had that in a while.

Today we had sergeant time training on a specific piece of equipment that is exclusive to our MOS. Once again the training was not conducted by a sergeant. Private First Class Hopkins gave the training. The majority of the information that we went over I already knew. There was a couple of things that I learned, but for the most part the training refreshed my memory.

I have a problem by being instructed by someone who is younger than me. I admit that I was not as attentive as I should have been. The information we went over is something that we do not come across every day, and if we do I know where to look for it. That is part of the reason why I was not being attentive.

Hopkins is very knowledgeable on the subject. He speaks in a very condescending manner, almost to the point to where you do not want to listen to him. Overall he did a good job, and took his class very seriously. That is something that NCOs should learn from. They are usually unprepared and boring when it comes to instructing. Nathan was very prepared and not the least bit boring.

We made another trip to Camp Essayons. We had to remove the remainder of the equipment there. The place is getting inspected tomorrow, and it had to be cleared of all equipment. Our lieutenant decided to start on the removal of the equipment the day before the inspection. Of course we did not finish. We didn't even get half way done. Hopefully is not that big of a deal. Had it been of some importance the lieutenant would have started clearing the room a week in advance. My guess is that we will continue removing the equipment tomorrow.

Friday September 23, 2005

My roommate and I were smoked at work today. Smoked is the term used in the military for reaching muscle failure. They makes us do pushups and a variety of other exercises until we reach muscle failure. Smoking us is supposed to help us learn our lesson. The smoking session were an every day occurrence during basic training. During AIT being smoked was less common. This has been my second smoking since I have been here. Smoking someone is even less common here, but it does happen.

The reason for being smoked was for sleeping on the job. When our section sergeant walked in he saw that my roommate was fast asleep. He immediately became infuriated and told us to get in the front leaning rest position. I assumed that he was only talking to my roommate so I stayed seated. I was not asleep, I was watching the news when the sergeant came in. He told me I had to get in the front leaning rest, because I was asleep as well. I told him that I wasn't, that I was watching the news. My back was to him so I don't know how he could have known that I was asleep. I did not argue. I did what he said and got in the front leaning rest position.

He went on, on how sleeping on the job is unacceptable. He said that there was plenty for us to do. He said that next time he was going to write us up. He did not care if we were asleep or not. If he perceived that we were asleep, that was going to be enough for him to write us up. He even threatened to take the television out. That way we would not watch movies. The movie watching should have not even been brought up, because the sergeants ask us for movies so they can watch movies at work as well. They are as guilty as we are when it come to watching movies at work.

I was very angry for being smoked for some thing I was not guilty of. If I was asleep I sure as hell would have admitted to it. I was not even sleepy like I usually am. I went to sleep at eight last night, so I got plenty of sleep. If he wanted to smoke me, he could have smoke me for watching television. He could have said that I was not being proficient. Smoking me because he perceived that I was asleep, that is ridiculous.

The leaning rest position used to be break me, but I have been in that position so many times that it does not phase me. I can stay in that position for a long time. I guess he noticed that being in the front leaning rest was not punishment for me, because he made me get in the dead roach position. In this position you lay on your back with hands and feet starched out in the air, as if attempting to touch your toes. They did not have this one in basic training and AIT. This position did hurt. After a while I was struggling to keep the position. I reached muscle failure.

He was also angry because I have not been cite certified. No one who came in after me has been cite certified either. That really did not apply to me because I can not site certify my self. Cite certification is a series of training on different aspects of our job and equipment. There is a specific amount of training that needs to be done before I can receive my thirty, sixty, and ninety day certifications. I have not even received my thirty days certification.

According to my roommate the training is supposed to be done by the section sergeant in order to be cite certified. My section sergeant, however; has endowed those responsibilities on every one who has been there before me. They are the ones responsible for making sure that I get cite certified. Everyone has left already. There are only three people left who can give me the training to become cite certified. I usually do not work with them.

Some how not being cite certified was still my fault. He said that I need to ask these individuals to give me the training required in order for me to become cite certified. Until recently I only worked with Parsons. Parsons came after me, he obviously can not training me. He has to be cite certified as well. The other times I have worked by my self.

Sergeants usually do not rationalize before trying to make a point. If it's anyone's fault for not being cite certified, it's his own. He should have scheduled better. Instead of putting me by myself and with Parsons, he should have scheduled me with some one who could have giving me the training.

I was watching on the news the evacuation for hurricane Rita. I was staying updated with development of this hurricane, because I have an aunt and uncle that live in the Houston area. Some of the people who were left with out homes from hurricane Katrina were in Houston, and know there is a hurricane headed there way. The hurricanes are following these people where ever they go. As if they hadn't had enough already.

I called my grandma and asked her if my aunt and uncle had evacuated. They evacuated the day before. What would have taken the three hours under normal circumstances took them seven hours. Seven hours is what it took them to get in to the Dallas are. I guess sitting in traffic for that long is worth it, if it makes the difference between survival and death.

I finally got a hold of Sheena today. I had called her on different occasions and every time I would get her voice mail. It was enjoyable talking to her, even though I had a hard time understanding her. There was a lot of static. She told me that she talked to one of our friends from AIT. He is in Korea as well, but I think he is further south. We are planning a trip to Mexico for when I go on leave. Hopefully our plans will go trough.

I received a letter from my sister today. In the letter she sent the sonogram picture of her baby. The picture is so clear, it is amazing to see how far technology has come along. He looks a lot like me when I was a baby. That can only mean on thing. He is going to be a cute baby. He would have either way because my sister is beautiful. I am very excited for her, my parents, and my self. It really blows that I will not be there to see him.

I decided to send my family post cards. I have a very big family, so I did not send every one a post card. I would have gone broke, had I sent everyone a post card. I figured that they would like to see a glimpse of what Korea looks like. The majority if the scenes in the post cards I have not seen myself. I will have to get around to cite seeing.

Saturday September 24, 2005

Nora and Dora are twins. They are my aunts that I grew up with. They are also only eleven months older than me. Ever since I can remember my grandparents have always been our neighbors. The three us grew up together. I have never actually considered them my aunts. We are around the same age, so they never played the aunt role. I never played the nephew role either. They were like my sisters. We have a special bond, or so I thought.

Today is their birthday, and I called them to congratulate them. I called Nora first, she had company so I did not talk to her very long. She asked me to call her back. Even though we talked for a very short period of time, there were a couple of awkward pause were no one said anything. I have not seen her in almost four months, and before that I did not see or talk to her much either. You would think that there would be plenty to talk about.

I called her back a couple of hours later. Her in-laws were there when I called. I know it would have been rude for her to stay on the phone, but she sees them more often that she will ever see me. I will not be back home until June, beside she is known for not being very polite. It is going to be a long time before she gets to see me again. I don't get to talk to her that often either. I thought that I would have priority, and that she would have excused her self to talk to me. Apparently she was somewhat distraught, because she did not get to spend time with me when I was home. She only saw me for about fifteen minutes. The fact that she blew me off contradicts her bewilderment from my absence.

The first time I called her he said that she would purchase a calling card and call me another time. I honestly doubt that. Since I have been here no one has bothered to call. I purchased my cell phone the first week I was here. She said for me to give her my phone number. I told her I did not have my cell phone with me, and that I did not know the number. I do not know the number, but I lied about not having my cell phone with me.

The second time I called her she said that she would call me back to the number my mom had given her. That says that she lied about not knowing my number. She had my number all along. I did not say anything, I simply agreed.

Sometimes I think that I am the only one who makes an effort in staying in touch with my family. They always say that they will buy calling cards to call me. I tell them that I will be the one to call them, because it is easier for me to call them. It is as easy for them to call me as it is for me to call them. My grandma, my mom, and my sister have managed to call me with no problem. I know that they will not call anyway.

They did not call me when I was in Georgia. Everyone knew my cell phone number then. They knew that I was off on the weekends. They definitely did not need a calling card to call me, because I had a local phone number. Even if they did have to but a calling card, I think that it is a small price to pay. The price can never be to high for staying in touch with your family.

I don't even know why I bother staying in touch with everyone. It is very disappointing to see the way that things turn out. I really expected more from them, especially from Nora. I do not know exactly what it was that I expected, but it sure was not getting blown off on the phone.

Maybe I am over reacting, but things have changed. I am not the same person that I was five years ago, and neither are they. I hear other soldiers talk about their families, and it seems like everyone is distant from their families. Some are even distant from there immediate family. I was always proud of how close I thought my family was.

My conversation with Dora was not as disappointing. In previous times that I have called her there has been plenty of awkward pauses. I think that everyone is caught up in their own life's. They have other things to worry about. They have families and problems of their own.

I should take it from them. I should focus more on my life and not worry about whether or not people stay in touch. I need to focus on what changes I need to make in my life, and not worry about existing in other people's life. Those who need to be in my life will be in my life.

My dad, mom, and sister are never to busy, they always place me before everyone and anything else. That is all that should matter. I am really pleased with my relationship with my sister, we are really close. My brothers are still kids, all they talk about is what they want for me to get them. When I do talk to them they are always attentive, never to preoccupied.

Sunday September 25, 2005

Last night we decided to go to Apache. We normally take the bus, which is less than a dollar. Last night they decided that we should take a cab. We got in the cab and had a conversation amongst each other, before we knew it the cab drive had taken the long way to the bar. By taking the long way to the bar he makes more money. We were also stalled in traffic, so that raised the fair even higher. We tried to tell him something, but he pretended he did not know what we were saying. They act stupid when it is convenient for them. When needed they make there point across any way possible.

I met another girl at Apache. Once again the language barrier was an issue. She did not know enough English and I did not know enough Korean to have a conversation. I am going to have to learn the language, but it is extremely difficult. The Korea language is very complex. I have been telling myself that I need to learn the language, but I never follow through with it.

After Apache we went to a club. This time around it was fun. We had girls to dance with. That is always a plus. Girls always make the night better. We weren't there to long. After a couple of drinks and some dancing we headed back.

We took another cab back to get on post. This time the cab driver gave us a flat rate of five dollars, regardless of how long or were he went through. The price was five dollars. We agreed that was much cheaper that the previous cab. I sat in the front seat and the other three sat in the back. It was two females an one male. The male and one of the females started making out in the cab. I thought that wasn't fair, so me and the other female started making out. Since I was in the front and she was in the back. I had to kneel on the seat and stretch towards the back. After that we switched, I started making out with the other female and vice versa. I wonder what the cab driver was thinking.

Today is my brother's birthday. Kevin turns thirteen. I wish I was home so I could celebrate with him. I can still remember being thirteen, things were much simpler then. At that age I was in a hurry to grow up and get older. Looking back now, I miss the days when I was younger, when there was less to worry about. I wish that I could go back to those days.

Monday September 26, 2005

Yesterday we were going to take a trip to Camp Casey. On our way to the bus stop I had to stop by the ATM, and so did the female soldier who was going with us. There she realized she did not have her debit card with her. After searching for it, she did not find it. We were stuck in the barracks. She came to the conclusion that she left her debit card at Mitchell's, but they did not open till later. By the time that Mitchell's opened it would have been to late to go anywhere.

We decided to chill in her room. She played the guitar for us. That was really soothing, but she could not play one complete song. This female is also an artist, so she showed us her drawings. I decided to draw in her sketch book while she cooked for us. We also drank alcohol like usual. This time around the atmosphere was different, it was a very creative atmosphere. I had not felt like that in a while. I haven't been drawing since high school. I was in the mood for drawing today.

Me and this female to a long walk. We talked about everything and anything. We have a lot of things in common, but we are very different in others. I felt like I connected with her. I have not connected with anyone since my arrival. She is a very genuine person, very sure of who she is. She has a good perspective and a great personality. I am looking forward to getting to know her more in depth. I am very attracted to her.

After she went to bed I stayed up with a newly made friend of mine. He had been drinking all day. We both practically finished a bottle of Absolute Vodka and Malibu Rum by ourselves. I felt pretty wasted by the time I went to bed. When I woke up this morning I actually felt worse than I did that night. All day I stayed in bed. I felt like shit. There is nothing else to do here than to drink. I am going to have to figure something out, because I do not want to become an alcoholic.

Tuesday September 27, 2005

I woke up very early this morning. I had to go to Yong Song. I am going to be here three days. I have to attend Seoul Tech Control University. Here I will learn everything I have to learn about working in tech control. These classes will help me to be more proficient in my job. I think that sending me now is exceedingly anomalous. I should have came here when I first arrived in Korea.

The classes were definitely not what I expected. I did not learn anything today. The classes that were taught by the Koreans I couldn't understand or hear them. The classes that were given by the soldiers were a joke. All they did was read a hand out. It was a waste of time. They were not prepared to teach. I was really looking forward to learning something. What they were going over was information that was useless. Even if I had understood what was being said that information was useless knowledge. We will never come across what they were talking about. I was extremely disappointed with the classes.

I also found out that I will be giving a class on the last day. I came here as a student. I was not expecting to have to give a class. How can I give a class on something that I do not even know my self. That proves how unprepared this three day training is going to be. I have until Thursday to familiarize myself as much possible on the topic, and then be able to teach others. I am always up for a challenge.

They did let us out of class early. I don't know if that was a good thing or a bad thing. We decided to go to a book store off post. For being a used book store the price on the books were some what expensive. The books were only two dollars cheaper than the original price. I purchased four books. I bought *The Adven-*

tures of *Tom Sawyer*, written by Mark Twain. I have heard a lot about George Orwell's novel *1984*. Everyone who has read the book says that it is an excellent book. I bought *Buffalo Wagons*, written by Elmer Kelton. When I was a senior in high school Elmer Kelton talked to us about being an author, and the challenges he faced trying to publish his first book. I was inspired by him. I wrote an article about him in the school newspaper. I read his first book *The Time it Never Rained*. He is a magnificent western writer, and that book was an excellent book. *A Tale of Two Cities*, by Charles Dickens was the other book I bought. I have only read one book by Charles Dickens which was *Great Expectations*, and it was a great book. I figured I would read another one of his books.

We stayed in the same barracks that we stayed in when I went to drivers training. This time it was on a different floor, and the rooms were not that obscene. I did not want to end up with another pubic hair in my mouth. The rug that was in the room looked like it had been vacuumed. The room actually looked like it had been cleaned before.

Thursday September 29, 2005

I gave my class today and it did not go that terrible. My class was on the DD Form 314, and Preventive Maintenance. The class was basically on how to schedule and record maintenance on the DD Form 314. I also went in on how often the maintenance is required on different tactical equipment. The class went smoothly. I could have done way better if I would have had more time to prepare.

Today I talked to my mom and dad. I told them how proud I am of them, and how much I appreciate what they have done for me. Growing up we seldom let are parents know how much they mean to us. Some people don't ever tell their parents how much they mean to them. We assume that they know. I do not want my parents to assume that I am grateful and that they mean the world to me. I want them to hear it from my own words.

Parents make mistakes, especially with their first child. They learned with me what it was to be a parent. They were not giving a manual that said this is how you will raise your son, what to do in this or that situation. They figured everything out their own. As a teenager I was annoyed by a lot of what they did. I questioned everything, but now I see that they only had the best intentions for me in mind. Teenagers do not see that. They only see what is directly on front of them. Sometimes we have to step back and look at the big picture. All I saw was that I had to be home at a certain hour, could not do this or that. I only saw the restrictions I had.

I have not been the best son. I have made parenting a challenge for them. There are many things I wish I could take back. That will never happen. What was said was said, and what was done was done. They only thing I can change is the future, and I will do my best to make them proud. I love my mom and dad. They are the best parents I could have ever had. I wish I could have had a better relationship with them when I was growing up. That is one of my biggest regrets, because my parents are awesome.

Friday September 30, 2005

Today we went to Everland, which is an amusement park here in Korea. It rained all day. The trip sucked. It had to rain the day that we decide to go on a trip. Most of the rides were closed because of the weather. There was nothing to do, but walk around. Everything that was indoors was opened, but that is usually the smaller kids stuff.

There was a lot of Korean students. The schools had a field trip that day. It was very weird, because they kept taking pictures of us. Now I know what celebrities feel like. It is very strange to have your picture taken by a stranger. At first we would pose with them, but after a while it became redundant.

Never did I imagine that I would run in to Castellenos, my battle buddy from basic training. I thought I was never going to see him again. It is a small world after all. Right as we were leaving a girl runs up to me and asks me if I remembered her. She was Burrus form basic training, she was in my platoon. She told me that she had seen me earlier but was not sure if it was me for sure. She told me that her and Castellanos are in the same platoon here in Korea. Their bus was parked by ours, so before leaving Burrus called him out of the bus and I said hi. It was nice to have ran into him, I was friendly and civil for a change. We did not talk for very long, maybe two minutes and that was it. I am glad to know that he is doing okay. If he survived being my battle buddy he can survive anything.

By the end of the trip I was soaking wet. My shoes and socks were drenched in water. I think we should get a refund, because the trip was not enjoyable. I had fun hanging out with two guys from Camp Casey, who are in our company. One of them is Mexican and the other is form the Dominican Republic. I was laughing the whole day. Latin people always have a good sense of humor.

5

October

Saturday October 1, 2005

Here lately I have been drinking entirely to much and last night was not the exception. There is this new female who recently became a part of our company, we had to do something to make her feel welcome. What better way to do that than by drinking beer. We blast the music, we listened to Juanes and the Kumbia Kings. No one understood what the songs were saying, but the beats are very rhythmic. We were asked to lower our music three times by the Katusa who was on CQ. We were a bit rowdy, and the music was blaring to top it of. We got tired of being told to lower the music so we went to Mitchell's.

I did not feel very comfortable at Mitchell's, because the majority of our NCOs were there drinking. Everyone else was trashed I figured I would look after them. Our first sergeant was there as well. He called me over to talk to me. Automatically I thought I had done something wrong. He told me to relax and to have a good time. He asked how I had been doing, and if I was staying out of trouble. I think I have done a pretty good job out of staying out of trouble.

Our first sergeant is a nice guy, very genuine. He is not the kind of person that demands respect, and because of his rank he can demand respect. He has a different approach to getting respect. He gives respect, even to the lowest ranking person. You always want to respect someone who respects you. Most people with higher rank try to make them selves feel superior, and make every one else feel inferior. No one wants to respect some one like that. Our first sergeant always speaks to people at their level. He is a great leader. You want to respect him because he shows you the same respect.

Sunday October 2, 2005

Yesterday a group of us went to Seoul. We missed the free bus, so we were forced to take a cab. We had to take to different cabs, because we all did not fit into one cab. The ride for the cab was forty dollars. I wished we wouldn't have missed the bus. Some one had to go to the restroom at the very last minute, and we did not make it on time.

When we got to Seoul we met in Yong Song at the post exchange. There I bought a sketch pad and some drawing pencils. I have not drawn in a very long time. I enjoy drawing, I figured that I should get back to drawing. I had an incredible art teacher when I was in high school, her name was Mrs. McCarson. I learned so many things from her, It would be a shame to let all of that go to waste I learned many different techniques and different drawing styles from her. Once she got a hold of me there was a major improvement in my art work. She also taught me how to paint with watercolors after learning that I ventured out into acrylics and oils. She is a extremely talented teacher.

After we were done shopping we went to get a hotel. I was not planning on staying the night, because I had to work today. I did not have a pass either, but neither did any one else. Out of the seven of us only one person had a pass. Only one person was legally able to stay off post. Apparently everyone stays off post without a pass and never gets caught. I figured I would take my chances. I called the other person who was going to be on shift with me today. I asked him to work the first six hours of the shift and I would work the last six. He agreed, so I decided to stay. It did not take long for them to convince me. Peer pressure is a bitch.

After that we all went out to eat. We went to an Indian restaurant. I had never had Indian food, it was delicious. I was starving because I had not eaten all day, maybe that is why the food tasted so scrumptious. I thought that the cooks were probably Koreans, but to my surprise they were actually people from India. The food was expensive but it was worth it. It was a very nice restaurant, except for our rude waiter. She didn't receive a tip from us. Hopefully that will teach her to be nice next time.

After we ate we went back to the hotel and started dinking. While the girls were getting ready we drank. I drew a picture of a horse while I was drinking. I did not come out that great. My drawing skills are a bit rusty, but I will get back to where I was. I could also blame it on the beer. The horse was still decent, but I know that I can do better.

Once the girls were dome getting ready we went to a bar. They had a special going, two drinks for the price of one. That's a bargain, considering how expensive drinks are at any bar. We had made a bet to see who could make out with the most people. There were three girls with us, I kissed all of them and I was at three. All the guys were at three. There were four of us so the girls were ahead.

They also kissed each other. That made them three points ahead of us. The special only lasted an hour. Once the drink special was over we went to the club.

We arrived at the club and everyone was having a good time. We were all dancing and enjoying our selves. Everyone else kept drinking. I stopped drinking once we got to the club. Some one had to stay sober. We lost all track of time, and before we knew it we were out past curfew hours. The majority of the people in the club were in the Army. There were quite a bit of soldiers violating the curfew regulations. We could not leave because we would get caught. Anyone who gets caught violating curfew gets an automatic Article 15.

I was not to worried about it, because there were so many people violating curfew. There were sergeants violating curfew, and they should be setting the example. We went back to the bar. The whole strip that we were on was a strip of bars and clubs. I saw people passed out on the ground. There was a guy trying to wake up his friend. The guy would not respond, he almost looked dead. He was gone. There were people stumbling every where, barely keeping themselves up. Couples were fighting, making out, and making complete fools of themselves. I had never seen so many people out of control in one place. I felt sorry for them, their expression looked empty.

People drink for many reasons. Some drink to have fun, some to forget, others to ease their pain, for various reasons. No matter how much you drown your sorrows with alcohol, when you wake up in the morning they will still be there. I looked at all these people and seeing them was depressing. I do not want to ever find myself looking the way those people looked. They are obviously not in control of their lives, I want to be in control of mine.

It was scary, that guy on the street could have been dead. He was not an American, he was Korean. I guess that why I did not bother to help him. No one seemed to care they were all preoccupied with getting drunk. The street was crowded with people and no one even asked if he was okay. Everyone was having what they called a good time. They whole setting was very disturbing.

We finally decided to walk back to the hotel. It was a little past three in the morning when we started walking back. Everyone was completely wasted. I think I was the only sober one. They were all struggling to walk straight. As we were approaching the hotel, a herd of military police came into view. My heart dropped, but we could not turn back. They had seen us already, we stayed calm and walk past them. We thought that if we acted normal they would not mess with us. We had already past by them and were crossing the road to get to the hotel.

Right when we were crossing the street someone grabs my arm jerking me back. It was a Korean police, and he was demanding to see my identification card. The military police notice what was going on, and they flocked to where I was. I was surrounded by at least ten military police. My heart sank. I was scared, I thought I was going straight to jail. There goes my military career, I am going to loose rank, and get an Article 15 I thought.

Everyone who I was with made it to the hotel. I could see that they were watching behind the bushes of the hotel. They were not being very discrete about it. I could see them peeping over the bushes. I was also mad, because they left me there by my self.

The Korean police still had a grip on me. The military police where asking to see my ID. I asked why the Korean police was grabbing me. They asked him to let me go, and they started questioning me. I handed them my Texas drivers license, but that was not the one they wanted. My hair cut gave me away, they new I was in the military. I had no choice but to show them my military ID. They made sure I knew in how much trouble I was.

They noticed that everyone else was looking from behind the hotel bushes. The rest of the military police rushed over there to question them as well. The girls ran into the hotel, but they were chased in there and brought back out side. I was escorted across the street and we were all being interrogated.

One of my friends was being a smart ass. They told us they were going to let us go, but since we were not cooperating with them they had no choice but to take us in. I thought they were going to take us in regardless. I thought that they had a zero tolerance when it came to curfew violations. They take that very seriously, and we also did not have a pass. One of the military police was about to call our first sergeant.

This whole time I was praying. I needed for God to get us out of this situation. The ramifications were going to be very severe if we were to have gotten caught. God must have been listening to me, because they let us go. Thank God my friend started cooperating with them other wise I would be in jail right know.

The reason they where behind the bushes was because they were debating whether or not to go and try to help me out. They were hoping that I would talk my way out of it. Half of them wanted to go help me, the others didn't. They did not know what to do. They could not walk much less make a decision about my situation. I can't blame them for leaving me there.

I was not able to sleep. I was afraid that I would not wake up in time to catch the bus and be able to make it in time to be at work today. For three hours I tossed and turned. Sometime during those three hours one of the guys got up and took a piss on the carpet by the window of the hotel room. I have no idea how that looked like the restroom to him. I did not tell him anything, it was not my room. I will just think twice before I lay on the floor of any hotel room.

I got up at seven this morning. I went to go check on people in the other room. When I was coming back to the room I noticed that one of the girls was in the close taking her pants off. Oh great, she must think that the closet was the bathroom, I thought. I closed the door to the room and stayed out side listening. I did not want to tell her anything. I did not want to embarrass her. Sure enough from outside the door I hear the piss trickling down. I could not believe it, and I thought I had seen it all. Once she was done I walked back in to the room.

I grabbed all my stuff. I took a cab to Yong Song, there I took the first bus to CRC. I made it back in time to take a shower and get ready to go to work. I am very tired. Work was not that busy so I was able to take a couple of naps. This is for sure the last time I pull this off. I do not want to risk getting in trouble, it's not worth it.

The drunks called me at work to see if I had made it back in time. I had to tell them what I witnessed. They had no recollection. They must have been completely wasted. How can someone think that the closet is the restroom? She could not believe it. While I was on the phone talking to her she went and looked in the closet. There was a wet spot. I laughed so much.

Today is my cousin Rafael's birthday, he turned twenty-one. I can still remember turning twenty-one, I counted down the days. I was legal. The first thing I did was buy beer. I did not have to worry about finding a buyer, I could know buy it myself. I was able to get into clubs and bars. That's when I started drinking more heavily, I was no longer restricted by my age. I would buy beer just because I could. It got old quick, especially when I had minors asking me to buy them beer. I always had asked people and would expect them to buy for me. Once they started asking me I did not like it. I was not going to risk getting in trouble for buying alcohol for minors. That's the worse part about being twenty-one.

Rafa and I grew up together. We had similar childhoods. We were close when we were kids. We fought a lot, but we got over it quickly. I would always throw rocks at him, when he made me mad. They always landed on his head. When he cuts his hair really short, all his scars become visible. I am responsible for all of them.

Rafa and I were close, he's like my brother. I could tell him anything, and he could do the same. The older we grew the further apart we grew. The only time that he would come around was when he could not find anyone else to buy him beer. He had his own friends I had mine. We grew up to be two very different people. There was a time that I disliked him. There was jealousy involved. I envied him, and for stupid stuff. Everything that was hard for me came very easy to him. Our family compared us a lot and that bothered me. People would say Rafa is this and that, they kind of threw it in my face that I was not like him. That is what their comments came across as. I usually stayed out of trouble, and he got into trouble. His dad would tell him why he could not be more like me. He hated that, we talked about it one day. Nobody wants to be compared to someone who you don't have any desire to be like. I think that's why we could not stand each other. Everyone wanted us to be more like the other.

Brothers fight, but at the end of the day they are still brothers. I know Rafa will always have my back regardless, and vise versa. I also know that I am still his favorite cousin. We have gotten over our differences. Even though we are very different, we still are close. We are alike in as many ways that we are different. You may not always get along with your family, but they will always be there.

Monday October 3, 2005

I called Rafa today, and wished him a happy late birthday. They had a barbeque for him on his birthday. I missed it, and I am sure that it will not be the last birthday party I will miss. Knowing that he is doing good is encouraging. I honestly wish him the best. I hope that he is successful in everything that he embarks. He has several hidden talents, I hope he finds a way to channel his creativity.

I start force protection tonight. I was not suppose to start until Wednesday, but the person on force protection had some other issues to tend to. I will be doing his last two days and he will be doing my last two days of force protection. This is the third month of force protection, and it's getting old already. I hope I don't have to do it next month.

Victoria and I are no longer talking through email. She sent me a message and I respond to it. She has not responded back. She has sent jokes, pictures, and stuff of that nature, but that is all. I think it is better of this way. She will come back around when she need some one to talk to, and I will be there. I also know that if I need someone to talk to that she will be there as well. We are friends, that's why we are in each others life. We do not have to constantly be in each others life to remain friends. I do not need her to be in my life like I thought I did. We are really close and some times that closeness can transmit the wrong signals. That is why there has been some confusion. I was kidding myself thinking that there was something between us. The only thing that is there is love for one another as friends. I guess I have always known that. I was holding on to something that was non existent. Romance always ends up messing up friendships, and that is one friendship that I am not willing to compromise. There is nothing between us other than a strong friendship.

Tuesday October 4, 2005

Force protection last night went by very rapidly. The first two hours on shift I read *Nicolae*, the third book in the *Left Behind* series. Tim LaHaye is an excellent author. I am hooked on these books. They get me to thinking about what lies ahead. I believe in what the books are about, and I do not want to be left behind. I will do every thing possible to make sure that does not happen.

The last two hours of force protection I slept. When I woke up it was time to go. I know that we are not supposed to sleep, but the first couple of nights are rough. It takes two or three night to get used it. Since it was cold outside we had the heater on inside the force protection building. It is more of a shack than a building. The warmth made it very cozy, very suitable for sleeping.

This morning the shift went by fast two. I was working with Miss Kim the Korean security guard. She is very fun to work with. She is funny, and makes force protection enjoyable. I also like flirting with her. She is good looking for someone her age. She is always talking, and it makes the time go by fast. When she runs out of things to say she will start asking questions. She likes to practice English. I help her with her English and she helps me with my Korean speaking skills. She is making more progress; however, I forget everything I learned by the next day.

Wednesday October 5, 2005

The weather at night gets somewhat cold. I have never been very fond of cold weather. I would much rather be hot than cold. Since it was so cold last night, we were all huddled inside the force protection shack. The heater made the cold bearable. We could not close the door, so it was not as warm as I would have like it to be.

I was trying to stay awake by reading a book. That did not work to well, all three of us fell as sleep. We were awakened by a drunk sergeant, he was incredibly pissed off. They always ask what unit we are from. Like everyone else he threaten to call our first sergeant. He went on and on about how we were not doing our job. I think that he could have gotten his point a cross without having to swear at us, but he was drunk. We were lucky that he did not call our first sergeant like he promised.

He said that someone could have come on post without us even knowing. Someone who could be of threat to us. We were compromising the security of everyone on post. He did have a point. I did not purposely fall a sleep, I passed out reading the book. Usually if someone is a sleep I will stay awake, I guess we all fell a sleep at the same time. We were not asleep very long, about ten minutes was all. Ten minutes is more than enough for someone to make his way in unknown.

He was an ass for the first ten minutes of time he was there. After he got done screaming and cursing he went on about his whole life basically. He started hitting on the security guard, and talked about his time in Iraq. He was being very comedic, making us laugh. Once he was done saying what he had to day, he dismissed himself. His final words were, "I have to go take a shit and go masturbate." We really did not need to know that.

During force protection this morning one of the sergeants told me that I had to be at the company at five. I was going to get promoted. Once I was done with force protection I went and got a hair cut. I wanted to look presentable in front of the whole company. I ironed a clean set of BDUs and shined my boots. It took more time getting ready than anything. We were promoted in five minutes. It is not a big deal going from private second class to private first class. The only difference is that I will be making more money. I could use an extra few bucks. I was not promoted for my meritorious performance as a soldier. The promotion is automatic after one year of service. Parsons was also promoted.

Today is one year exactly, the day I left home to go to the MEPS station in Amarillo. My emotions were more on edge the day I felt to come to Korea than on that day. I was excited to start on this new journey that is the Army. I was looking forward to start all over. Joining the Army gave me hope to make things right for myself. I was ready to be challenged mentally and physically. I needed discipline in my life. I screwed up everything else, I was determined to make the Army work for me.

The night before I had a farewell dinner at my house. The majority of my family was there. It was a peculiar feeling that night. Everyone was not being themselves. My aunts cried. I was not moved by their tears, I was ready to leave Big Lake. Their tears was prove that they cared, but I did not want anyone to be sad. I wasn't sad, I was excited. It was going to be a complete different experience. Most of all I wanted to do something where my family would be proud of me. I want to be proud of myself.

The last person I spoke to that night was Victoria. She did not want me to join, but I needed to do this for me. No one's words had moved me that day, but when I talked to Victoria that changed. I was used to listening to her voice almost every day. For the past four years in my life she has always been there. Leaving her behind felt like I was leaving a part of me behind. Now she is extremely proud of me, and that means a lot to me.

Thursday October 6, 2005

One year in the Army. This day a year ago I had no idea what to expect. This day a year ago was the first time I was on an airplane. It was not the smoothest ride either, my hands were sweating. I was nervous, and prayed that the airplane would stay in the air. The possibility of the plane crashing always crosses my mind when I board an airplane. I still have not gotten used to flying. I feel that I always have to be in control of my environment. In the air you have no control over anything. The only one who has control is the pilot. To place my safety on a stranger is very uncomfortable.

When I arrived at reception I knew that my life would no longer be the same. The screaming and yelling was the first thing I heard when I got off the bus. I had prepared my self for the worse, it turned out not being all that harsh. The two months of basic training were actually fun. The drill sergeants did not get to me, I knew that they were going to yell and get in my face. That is what basic training is about. The times it did get unpleasant I would tell myself that it would be over soon. They could not keep us in the front leaning rest all day. They had to let us go to lunch. There was always somewhere to go. There was always something scheduled, no punishment was going to last to long. They tried to expose your weakness and fears. We had to face them and over come them. Basic training is actually overrated.

This year has been eventful, to say the least. It has been a challenge. I am trying to deal with and come to terms with the fact that I will be missing out on many things. I am sacrificing being away from my family. I've learned to have to deal with people, I do not necessarily care for. I have learned to remain silent. There are times that I have to bite my tongue and except things. Silence is the best reply to the ignorant. There are things that we have no control over, but I have found that we have control over the outcome. We control how were are going to react. We chose how much of an impact tribulations have on us. I will not let things that I cannot control tear me apart. I have learned more about myself here. There are things that used to be important to me and now seem petty.

I talked to Gabriel today. He is getting married after all. I wish him luck, marriage is a big step to take. Being in the military will complicate things. When something is real it will endure everything. There is nothing love cannot endure, when it's real. I question myself when it comes to Ali. I feel that I let a good girl go. I pushed her away. If what we had was real, if our feelings towards each other are real, everything will work out in the end. Destiny will find a way to bring us together again. If we were not meant to be, what is left will fizzle into only a memory of something we once shared. If our love is real it will be fueled by the hope of one day reuniting. I have to wait and see.

Friday October 7, 2005

When you praise someone, there will always be someone there to bring that person down. If you ever want to know something negative about someone tell someone how great that other person is. They will go into how appearances can be deceiving, and dish everything bad that they know about that person. We like to hear what corrupted things people do. We focus on them, and they become the topic of the days gossip. We focus so much on other people an make sure everyone knows what they have done. We do this to make the terrible things we do seem less trivial. See we all do things that we are ashamed of, and we dig for peoples dirt to tell our self that others have done worse.

Life is not about what we did or how we were. The only thing that matters is what we are doing to change, what matters is who we are trying to become. There is evil in every one, but there is also righteousness in everyone. If we step back and move our sight from what is wicked, we will see the light. Sometimes our light is dim. There are different things that dim peoples light, everything that we are ashamed of will diffuse our light. If we search deep within other people, deep with in ourselves, we will see the light.

There is one female I said I would never hang out with again. When I met her I did not like how she was. I have gotten to know her, and I got to see who she really is. I enjoy hanging out with her now. She is funny, she is a good listener, a good cook, and she cares. I see her light.

When I heard about the sergeant and his issue with child pornography, I was appalled. I really did not care to socialize with him because of what I knew. After getting to know more about him the more he does not fit in the image that I had of him. This could all be false. The person who said this about him could have said it to cover up his guilt. Maybe he was the one who is into child pornography. He incriminated someone who could be innocent. I choose to believe that he is innocent, there is a very tangible kindness about him. I do not think that he is that type of person, and I don't care to know either. I saw his light.

Since I have been here I have been warned about different people. When someone tells us something negative about someone those words get engraved in our minds. When ever we come across that person, we only see what we were told. Half of the time what we hear is false, exaggerated, or completely thrown out of proportion. I don't want not to get to know someone because of what I have heard. I want to give everyone a fair chance. I want to search for their light.

There are people here that I don't like. I don't dislike them because of what I've heard, but because of who they are. They are not completely villainous, they choose not to let people in. Some people will not let you in until they see your light. Sometimes personalities clash. Maybe they are blinded by what they hear or what they see. They have not stepped back far enough to see the real me. Frankly I do not care to get to know everyone. I like being a loner, and hopefully they will never step far back enough. God will place people in my life who need to be in my life. God sees my light.

Four months I have been here. The time here has gone by fast, before I know it I will be going home. I like it here, it is not that terrible. There are moments when it really sucks. Regardless of were we find our selves there will be moments that are unpleasant. I have to take the good with the bad. I have eight more months to go, and I plan to make the best out of it. The Army is a way to learn about what you are capable of doing. There is always something to be learned. I have entertaining memories so far. The nights at Apache are memorable. I've even had great times working in tech control. I have eight more months to go, and I plan to make the best of it. The first four months in my first duty station have been enjoyable. Army life has been an incredible opportunity for me to start all over.

978-0-595-37598-1
0-595-37598-7

Made in the USA
Middletown, DE
23 January 2019